LIKE AN EVER-FLOWING STREAM

LIKE AN EVER-FLOWING STREAM

Meditations on Justice and Peace

Based on Readings from the Old Testament

JOHN CARMODY

THE UPPER ROOM
Nashville, Tennessee

Like an Ever-Flowing Stream

The serigraph on the cover entitled "Silver Stream" is by James Hagen/AUSTIN PUBLISHING CO.

Cover and Book Design: Roy Wallace
First Printing: November 1987 (5)
Library of Congress Catalog Card Number: 87-050701
ISBN: 0-8358-0567-0

Printed in the United States of America

For JOHN and CATHERINE GAMMIE

CONTENTS

PREFACE *9*

I. TORAH

1. Stewardship *15*
2. Suffering *20*
3. Murder *25*
4. Preservation *29*
5. Justice *33*
6. Holiness *37*
7. Jubilee *41*
8. Hearing and Teaching *45*
9. Destruction and Love *50*
10. Life and Death *55*

II. PROPHETS

11. Divine Rule *63*
12. Personal Sin *68*
13. Prophecy *72*
14. Messianic Peace *77*
15. Punishment *82*
16. Victimhood *86*
17. Inner Renewal *90*
18. False Pastors *94*
19. Judgment *99*
20. False Trust *104*

III. WRITINGS

21. The Law *111*
22. Foresakenness *116*
23. Worship *121*
24. The Silence of God *125*
25. The Champion *130*
26. Righteousness *135*
27. Love *140*
28. Vanity *145*
29. Timing *150*
30. Wisdom *155*

PREFACE

I think of this book as a complement to my book of New Testament meditations on peace and justice, *The Quiet Imperative,* published last year by The Upper Room.

Working with the Old Testament has been a challenge, albeit a very rewarding one. First, there is the matter of the complexity of the text, which modern scholarship can make quite daunting. I have reflected this scholarship in my exposition, assuming that many readers need help (more than they would with the New Testament) if they are to situate a given text correctly. Second, there is the earthiness and irony of many narratives. I have come to love the Bible's own love of human complexity and imperfection. The Bible shows great patience with recalcitrant human nature and great awareness of the intricacy of human motivation. If ever one wanted a book to confound literalism and fundamentalism, the Hebrew Bible is it.

Third, the Old Testament has come to serve me as a bridge to fuller love of Jewish religious experience. What impressed me when I first read the tales of the Hasidim is even clearer in the stories of Adam and Eve, of David and Bathsheba. It runs in the cynical judgments of Qoheleth and exults in the eroticism of the Song of Songs. This is the gamble, the trust, that God has made us not angels but people of flesh and blood, of passion as well as brains, of sweat and dirt as well as sweet patience, white linen, and bay rum.

Last, the God of the Bible so passionately yet patiently wants mercy rather than sacrifice and justice rather than vengeance that the Bible becomes the judge not only of our tolerance of injustice but also of its own excesses and misjudgments. When Israelite bloodlust or priestly legalism or sexist depreciation of women starts to cavort, the deeper passages—Second Isaiah, Jeremiah, Job—rise up to shout no. Even if it occurs in God's own book, such failure to adhere to God's standards of justice and love allows us to write the author of the given passage off. One has to admire such a self-critical book. One has to love its humility and goodness. So this return to the Old Testament has been a wonderful experience for me personally. My recent studies have convinced me that the Old Testament is funny, irreverent, and deadly serious about equating the values of our faith with the justice we display in our daily lives.

A few terms perhaps deserve explanation. *Torah* can name either the first five books of the Old Testament or the whole of divine instruction. *Prophets* actually collects not only oracles and interpretations by the Israelite prophets but also historical materials. Still more disparate, *Writings,* the third portion of the Hebrew Bible, includes poetry, wisdom literature, apocalyptic, and other genres. The texts I have selected only skim the surface. Many others also offer good materials for meditating on peace and justice.

My viewpoint is explicitly Christian, although I don't emphasize any superseding of the Old Testament by the New, and I don't pursue prophetic anticipations of Jesus at great length. What I do frequently develop are the further thoughts suggested by comparison of a given text with the teachings or example of Jesus.

I use the now fairly common designations *B.C.E.* (Before the Common Era = B.C.) and *C.E.* (Common Era = A.D.).

Readers wishing quick access to the sort of scholarship on which I have depended might begin with the three following works:

Achtemeier, Paul J., ed., *Harper's Bible Dictionary.* San Francisco: Harper & Row, 1985.

Gottwald, Norman K., *The Hebrew Bible: A Socio-Literary Introduction*. Philadelphia: Fortress, 1985.

Knight, Douglas A., and Tucker, Gene M., eds., *The Hebrew Bible and Its Modern Interpreters*. Philadelphia: Fortress, 1985.

The exposition follows the order of the canonical Hebrew Bible, taking seriously its traditional division into Law, Prophets, and Writings. Each part of the Bible has important things to say about justice and peace and their constituents or conditions, but Jewish tradition has always accorded the Law, or Torah, more honor than the Prophets, and the Prophets more honor than the Writings. The theme in the first portion of the text is the guidance of Israel's Creator and Liberator on the path that is straight. The theme in the second portion is the word of God given through the prophets for the cure of evil times. The theme in the third portion is the wisdom inculcated by long experience of oppression and the divine silence. Collectively, these three thematic emphases suggest that revelation and suffering alike make justice and peace God's own signature.

My thanks to Charla Honea of The Upper Room for sponsoring this project; to my wife, Denise, for deflating support; and to those who have stimulated my interest in the Old Testament in recent years, especially Bob Cohn, John Gammie, Stuart Lasine, and Jerry Unterman. May peace visit all their houses and justice attend all their venturings.

I

Torah

The Guidance of Israel's Creator and Liberator

1

Stewardship

Genesis 1:26–31

I must confess that beginning with the beginning of the Bible was difficult. I had to shake off the assumption that I had heard the creation account so many times that certainly it could hold no surprises. I had to fight the prejudice raised during studies of the ecological crisis that the supremacy accorded human beings is a potent factor in the history of our devastation of the environment. And, above all, I had to let myself be again seduced by the charm and depth of the biblical myths, by the Bible's preference for doing theology by telling stories. Only after these first adjustments could I start to glimpse where the scholarly expositions I had consulted ought to be taking me.

This Genesis text is one of the most famous in the Bible. Current scholarship suggests that it was composed by Jewish priests around 500 B.C.E. after the return from exile in Babylon. The fifty years following the deportation of the elite of the land to Babylon were the most traumatic in Israelite history. Even though the Temple in Jerusalem was rebuilt in the years 520 to 515, the books of Ezra and Nehemiah suggest that the people were in great danger of losing their identity. One of the things the priestly writers surely were trying to do was to place all of human life, but especially that of the people descended from Abraham, in the safe context of a creation well regulated by God from the beginning. Many of the main aspects of the text gain a sharper focus when we consider them in this light.

First, there is the security that comes from the explicit affirmation that God made humanity most purposefully. Men and women can be comforted by thinking that both their existence and their nature derive from a choice made in heaven at the beginning. Moreover, the intelligence, love, and power of God are reflected in human beings' eyes. Since God is the source of the whole of creation, and so the guarantor of its meaning, human beings are like God in assuring the earth its order and meaning. What we do here below, the author is saying, is at least a faint picture of what God does above. The fullness of human being that "male and female" suggests—the fertility, complementarity, and sharing—is a clue to the fullness of divine being. What makes human beings special on earth (our capacity for "dominion," which we might best understand as "responsibility") is what makes God unique. For the Bible God is the One who bears final responsibility for the goodness of creation, the hopes of Israel, and the grace of Jesus the Christ.

From the blessing and command of verse 28, traditional Jews derived a sense of obligation to marry and raise children. Apart from some of the Essenes, a separatist group that flourished from about 150 B.C.E. to 70 C.E., Judaism had no ranks of deliberate celibates. Sticking to the first chapter of Genesis, we may note that there is no mention of death or afterlife framing the command to be fruitful, multiply, fill the earth, and subdue it. At this point, creation and fertility are simply good in themselves. The point is that life, freshly made by God, has an imperative to communicate and increase. As God has communicated and started the multiplications involved in creation, so human beings are to come together and produce. Natural and ordinary as this process must have seemed by the year 500 B.C.E., the author of Genesis 1 wanted to dignify it, even to consecrate it, by explicitly making it part of how God had brought humanity about. Indeed, Genesis 1 makes fruitfulness the first divine command uttered to the images whom God fashioned and blessed.

Second, the responsibility that human beings have for the rest of the earth extends to both animal and vegetable life. Those who are images of God and able to receive God's commands are responsible for what happens to the earth, the fish of the sea, the birds of the air, and all the rest of animal life. The implication seems to be that if these other creatures were not to flourish, God would ask an accounting of human beings. When we reflect that economic depression in Israel after the Exile was such that many people were poor and many crops and beasts were languishing, we may suspect that the priestly writers had an explicit contrast in mind. What ought to have been, according to the Creator's designs, was not happening. If the Israelites were to get things back into the good order that God had intended, they would have to assume responsibility and set their shoulders to the wheel.

A note of nonviolence and restraint appears in verse 29 in the strong suggestion that God intended humanity to be vegetarian. It is explicit that human beings have the plants and fruits for food, as the beasts do, while no mention is made of any right to use the animals as food. In the story of Noah in chapter 9, the priestly authors describe a God-given permission to eat animal flesh, although not blood. This presumably is one of the main reasons for the "dread" which, according to Genesis 9:2, the beasts and birds will feel toward human beings. Before repeating the command to "be fruitful and multiply" (9:7), God conjoins this abstention from animal blood with a prohibition against killing—bloodshed—among human beings. The whole tenor of the permission to eat flesh (9:3), therefore, is negative and threatening. The dietary laws that developed in Judaism reflected these biblical sentiments. In killing, preparing, and eating food, human beings were to distance themselves as much as possible from cruelty, bloodshed, and anything else that might cause them to forget the high value God placed on all life.

The end of Genesis 1 rings with the goodness that the Creator found in creation and makes human beings the pinnacle of God's handiwork. After making humanity in the divine image on what the Bible pictures as the sixth day of creation, God rests. Certainly the priestly authors had in mind the Sabbath that Israel had long celebrated, and certainly the account is calculated to make this regular day of rest an image of what the Creator did in the grand work that gives all human labor its frame.

The assurance that creation, definitely including humanity, is very good in God's sight should have made a lie of any attempt to despise human nature. There is no hint in the priestly account of creation that human beings are disobedient, twisted, pridefully aspiring to be like gods, or otherwise possessed of good reasons to feel shame. The view here is that they are creatures of unique dignity; they are reflections of God whose responsibility for the earth makes them preeminent and whose rich procreation is God's full will.

What does all of this suggest for our present-day concerns about peace and justice? If one comes to Genesis 1:26–31 with both Christian faith and a desire to move the nations away from war and toward fairer sharing, what thoughts and directives come to mind? Certainly the first thought may well be that taking responsibility for the fate of the earth is a God-given call and right. Genesis 1:26–31 slams a solid door against all species of irresponsibility and despair, against those who think evolution is a blind process with no ultimate meaning as well as those who eagerly await a nuclear holocaust that would lift up the elect into God's sky. The earth has been given into our hands that we may imitate the divine creativity and help the earth to prosper. The ecosphere lies on our consciences as something we did not make, and we must rule or guide wisely. To threaten the earth with nuclear winter—the blocking out of the sun by the clouds of dust caused by nuclear explosions and the consequential languishing of all life—is to contradict diametrically what was in the priestly view the command that humanity received from its earliest establishment. To interpret the dominion of human beings over nature as a license to plunder it and bring about deadly disorder utterly mocks the Creator's intent.

Thinking thoughts such as these, Christians and others who take the Bible as a privileged wisdom about how human beings may live well or as a privileged disclosure of what the divine mystery is about on our behalf often speak of stewardship. We hold the goods of the earth in trust for the sake of all of humanity and all of the earth's creatures. The earth is not ours to trash and deface and overtire. It is a trust—a gift of the One who first set the stars spinning and still breathes in each infant's cry. The peace and justice to which Christians are called is framed from the outset by the gratuity and mystery of creation. We will not see the order, proportions, or the imperative of creation rightly until we kneel at the verge of God's sabbath and call the whole of creation very good.

How does human responsibility reflect the divine nature?

What are realistically ideal relations between human beings and the rest of creation?

How seriously should we take the affirmation of Genesis that God saw human nature and creation as very good?

2

Suffering

Genesis 3:14–19

After their disobedience, the primary couple, Adam and Eve, learn from God the sorry consequences. Most biblical scholars consider this text part of the Yahwist source (abbreviated "J"), which analysis suggests is the oldest of the traditions now incorporated into the Bible. Perhaps 925 B.C.E. would be a good date at which to place the consolidation of this tradition (parts of it may be hundreds of years older). If so, it comes from the golden age of Israelite prosperity, when the kingdom of David was in the hands of his son Solomon. No doubt the sober reflections of the text would be relevant in any time, but it is intriguing to think that they were circulating precisely when Israel would have been most tempted to puff itself up with pride.

My teacher of biblical literature at Stanford, Ted Good, made his reputation with a study of irony in the Old Testament. Again and again, he would point out the humor and self-deprecation of the text. One of the problems that Jews have with the New Testament, he and several of my Jewish classmates noted, is that it is seldom humorous. True, there is Zacchaeus up in the tree and the retort of the man born blind to the Pharisees who are badgering him, but, compared with the Old Testament, the New Testament seems grim indeed. No doubt this is because, as many commentators point out, the Gospels are largely passion narratives with brief introductions and epilogues. The Old Testament, less intensely focused, has more space, both psychic and physical, to play around.

Such play, I hasten to add, is serious. The Bible is seldom, if ever, frivolous. But the this-worldly focus of so many passages, the lack of concern with an afterlife, seems to have made the foibles and conceits of human beings laughable. So Elijah asks the priests of Baal whether their great deity, who has to that point been a no-show, has gone aside to relieve himself. So Rachel steals the household gods of her father, Laban, and sits on them while supposedly menstruating to show what the Bible thinks of such idols. So Jacob, the wily cheater, is himself cheated by Laban. The prophetic and wisdom literature also brims with wit and reflectiveness. I have been consoled after reading such grim passages as Genesis 3:14–19 by recalling this larger framework of irony, thinking that it suggests touches of the divine compassion. No matter how much God despises human evil, God finally clothes our nakedness, perhaps shaking Adam and Eve affectionately as they leave the garden.

The intent of the verses seems clear enough: The authors are wrestling with the problem of human suffering. And it is not so much particular woes and hurts that hold their attention as it is the pervasive pain that racks humanity through and through. Something has gone very wrong for human beings always and everywhere to have to endure great pain and see their hopes shrivel. The strong emphasis on the goodness of creation that we noted in the priestly account of creation may well have been a deliberate effort to counterbalance the grimness in the older Yahwist tradition. True enough, the Yahwist shows touches of humor and irony. Taken in its full extension, this strand of Israelite memory and imagination is appealingly earthy and vital. But in Genesis 3:14–19 the authors are allowing themselves to face what philosophers might call the grim "existentials" that play in every person's life. Each woman is marked by her capacity to conceive children and raise the next generation. Each man is marked by an association with wresting a living from nature and his fellows. Both sexes return to the earth from which they were drawn, and this mortality marks them through and through.

Obviously, the cultural assumptions behind this account of human suffering lead the authors to deal in certain sexual stereotypes, and we should not get sidetracked by them. Men carry just as many implications in their sexuality as women do, and women are just as marked by their work as men. The gross point of the story is that human existence is hard; it is a struggle so demanding that we are bound at times to wonder what we have done wrong. It is this gross point that should get most of our attention, for in it lies a great basis for the compassion on which all significant work for peace and justice depends.

Genesis 3:14–19 does not deny that life is good and human time often is joyous. It does not deny that the majority of women quickly write off the pains of their labor in their happiness that the miracle again has happened and a child has been born. It is no enemy of the truth that creative work brings both men and women much of their reason to be. But Genesis, like all of our linear expressions, can only say one thing at a time. Here it is saying that suffering goes to our marrow, and we shall never be wise unless we reckon with this elementary fact.

For the Yahwist we come from dust and unto dust we must return. What takes us from dust is the breath of God; as soon as we lose that breath we wither and fall. The Yahwist knows nothing of an immortal soul or a body bound for resurrection. The wonder riveting his or her attention is that here and now, for this brief shining hour, God has quickened blood and nerves that may know great pleasure but more certainly will know pain. This is the way it is. Deep in the origins of human existence, back in the very first mold, the absurdity of pain and frustration entered in. The striking thing is that the temptation to blame God, which the serpent represents, is so thoroughly rejected. If something is wrong with the way things are in creation or in human affairs, the fault is either something we cannot assign or something we must accept as lying on our own heads.

By the time that this account was written, Israel had considerable experience of its God. At the beginnings of the special history that the Bible celebrates lay Abraham, the source of all the chosen people. At the crucial juncture lay Moses, through whom God worked liberation from Egypt and struck the special covenant. And most recently there had been David, the fully fallible king, whose accomplishments raised the possibility that God would never forswear the divine promises to be compassionate, merciful, longsuffering, and abounding in steadfast love.

This reading of Israelite history as punctuated and structured by saving acts of God on the people's behalf buttressed the walls of a faith strong enough never to blame God. Later we shall see another chapter on this theme when we study the arguments of Job. But right here, in a part of scripture that Israel always gave higher status than Job, there is no question of God's being responsible for the twistedness of human existence. The serpent crawls on his belly and eats dust in a pithy expression of what the Bible thinks of attempted seductions. The woman is forced to face her womb, and the man is forced to face his sweat. Sovereignly, the Creator tells all three that their disharmony with the divine order has won them severe and appropriate punishment. Right after the end of our text God will clothe the couple in a touching gesture of concern. In the text itself, however, the entire tenor is stern: This is how it is; get used to it.

There will be other places for us to defend the rights of the utopian imagination that refuses to accept human suffering and thereby generates a great deal of hope. There will be places, as well, for us to muse about resurrection and divine life. This seems the place to think about the sufferings of work, family life, growing old, and dying as a sentence laid on us by God, the One who made the universe and sees to its workings, ultimately for our benefit. The corollary might be that, if we could get this elementary yet difficult matter right, we might do much better at peace and justice.

The victims of war (un-peace of all sorts) are right and winsome to struggle to try to end the fighting and gain an honorable resolution. At home, on the job, in the international arena, we applaud the peacemakers and think them children of God. While war obtains, however, there is no profit in denying it. While injustice rambles on, Pollyannas and politicians who deny it do us all great harm. We have somehow to accept the fact that suffering is ordinary, statistically probable. Without making disease more significant than health, or war more significant than peace, or lying more significant than honesty, we yet have to see all such negatives for the commonplace entities they are. God has made a world in which it is so easy for nature and human beings to collide, act irresponsibly, and refuse to be what they might that suffering is a virtual certainty.

For faith, the implication is that God tolerates such certain suffering in view of something that to God's mind makes it acceptable. Judaism has used the story of the binding of Isaac (Gen. 22) as a help toward writing God such a carte blanche of trust, and Christianity has used the crucifixion. Both symbols tell the mind it must radically question its assumptions and own up to the mystery of evil and the greater mystery of God. Both symbols imply that God can bring about resolutions that save the divinity from initial appearances of cruelty and lead human beings to confess, in all honesty, that they simply do not know the proportions of the cosmic drama. With such confession we humans simply have finally to say yes, we will stay in a game we cannot win on our own, we will continue playing by rules we never fully understand, or we will say no, it is too much for us to bear and our outrage or fatigue has done us and "God" in.

Genesis 3:19–24 does not deny these ramifying implications, but it does treat the problem of suffering more concisely. "Bear it," the Yahwist says. "Take up your love and your work, if need be like crosses. God knows what you have to undergo, and in some ultimate sense God asks it. You came from dust and live only by God's breath. Only God's breath (Spirit) can fully transform your pain and mortality."

What do work and childbearing suggest about sexual stereotypes?

How should the inevitability of suffering shape our conception of justice?

Why does God tolerate suffering?

3

Murder

Genesis 4:8–13

The Yahwist, to whom this passage also tends to be assigned, is nothing if not realistic. Just as the previous chapter confronted the bedrock sufferings that afflict human beings, so this chapter confronts one of our worst potentials. We can become so disordered and so closed in on ourselves and heedless of the goodness of God's creation that we burst out in murderous rage or envy. If we take murder as a symbol of humanity at its most warped, studying murder may tell us volumes about what nurturing life toward peace and justice requires.

We should note, however, that the Bible is more sophisticated than to sketch for Cain, the first murderer, a simple-minded psychological profile. Since Cain was the firstborn of Adam and Eve, perhaps he carried special burdens of responsibility. He eventually became deadly envious of Abel, the second-born. It is likely that the Yahwist is well aware of sibling rivalry, for the story of Jacob and Esau (see especially Gen. 25–28) in all probability stems from the Yahwist tradition.

A further point to note is the different and competing occupations that Cain and Abel undertook. That Abel was a shepherd and Cain a farmer certainly implies that the story wants to make the antagonism between these two groups, who tend to have different senses of how land should be used, something extremely ancient. Why God should have accepted the offerings of Abel and rejected those of Cain is never explained. Either the text wants to imply that shepherds are closer to God than farmers or it wants to assert the freedom of God to act as God pleases. We do get a hint in 4:6–7, where God addresses Cain, that Cain has done something that prevented his gaining favor with God. We also get God's assurance that if Cain does well he will be accepted. Genesis continues, therefore, to shield God from any charges that the sins of human beings come home to roost through divine mistreatment. (Note that in 4:7 sin is pictured as an animal just waiting to spring upon Cain and devour him.)

Cain apparently chooses to nurse his anger and open the door to sin rather than to accept the freedom to choose to do what God wants and in so doing remain faithful to the primary imperative of his own conscience—to find a way to submit himself to God in peace. The parables of Jesus make the point that God's justice and human justice often employ different standards. God does no injustice to the laborers hired early in the day in giving those hired late the same wage (see Matt. 21). God pays those hired early all that had been promised them. For the first group to envy the good fortune of those hired late and recoil from the generosity of God toward the others is a sign of the distance they must travel before they will understand the kingdom of God. So, too, the parable of the prodigal son (Luke 15) makes it plain that the grumbling of the elder son is a sign that he simply does not understand the justice that pure love tends to generate.

Genesis does not spell out this logic as clearly as Jesus does in the parables of the Synoptic Gospels, but Genesis certainly does have God tell Cain that he should get control of his anger and make certain that his soul stands open to accepting whatever God requires of him. But Cain will not muster this measure of discipline, self-denial, and obedience. He will not face the deficiencies in himself. He has to project onto Abel the disorder that causes his pain and make Abel his enemy. Much of the psychology of sin is concentrated in this so brief sketch of Cain. Again and again people wound others because they cannot or will not come to grips with their own failings and make the changes that honesty requires.

When Cain gets Abel out into the field his envious rage boils over into murder. The Bible thinks that the land belongs to God, as we shall see when we consider the Jubilee prescribed in Leviticus 25. Genesis has already implied that both Cain and Abel accept God's sovereignty over the land, for both shepherd and farmer bring firstfruits and firstlings of the flocks to God as a sacrifice, an expression of their awareness that all increase comes from God. But in the field that God has given for life Cain lets the animal rush of sin use him to bring death. Immediately, God asks Cain (conscience afflicts Cain with) the primordial social question, "Where is Abel your brother?"

Cain is still turned from God, curved in on himself, and so a liar. His answer to God and conscience is another spark of genius on the Yahwist's part, for it epitomizes what makes social justice so difficult. Cain, who knows very well where Abel is, pretends not to know. He will not accept responsibility for murdering his brother, just as he would not accept responsibility for bringing sacrifices that God could not accept or responsibility for controlling his envy and anger. Cain is precisely the opposite of the image of God that the priestly account of creation described. Where human beings made in the image and likeness of God are above all to bear responsibility for the creation that has been put into their hands, Cain is irresponsible to the point of murdering his brother and polluting the land with blood.

Cain's surly addition to his lie about his brother only moves him further away from God's image: "Am I my brother's keeper?" The answer to this rhetorical question clearly is, "Yes, damn right you are!" It was with some amazement, therefore, that I once watched a panel of experts on foreign affairs debate the question of social responsibility and heard many of them deny any responsibility, answering the question, "No, we are not our brothers' keepers." A few of the naysayers realized that this put them at odds with Genesis and on the side of Cain, but this seemed a matter of concern only on the level of public relations. It is still bad form in the United States to be found contradicting the Bible. My amazement lingered even after I heard the fuller explanation for the dissenters' position and agreed that, taken simplemindedly, the notion of social responsibility could lead to paternalism, interfering in others' affairs, or keeping other people (e.g., third-and fourth-world nations) from developing their own responsible citizenship and their own political institutions. For the dissenters really were saying that, in the final analysis, we are atoms who exist independently and have no responsibilities for one another (as we would have if our human being were intrinsically social). These panel members really were opening the door to the law that might makes right or the policy that I may neglect others as much as I want as long as I do not actively hurt them or unduly infringe upon their freedoms.

Mencius, one of the most revered authorities of ancient China, agreed with Genesis that we bear responsibility for one another. He argued that it is simple, common instinct to rush after an infant who is headed for an open well to keep the child from tumbling in. For Mencius this instinct revealed a bedrock solidarity among human beings and a bedrock goodness in human nature on which all politics depends. How much of our current warfare and injustice flows from our rejection of the view of human nature found in Genesis and Mencius? How much of our current suffering stems from the ironic fact that, although we have had centuries more of human experience to ponder and although we are immeasurably more advanced technologically, we are palpably less wise?

At any rate, Genesis assures us that blood we shed in murder cries to God from the ground. Indeed, it says that the earth itself curses those who pollute it by bloodshed. For Genesis, the earth is a living entity, sacral and not to be polluted. Cain's sin makes Cain an alien to the earth. He must wander as a fugitive. Cain, to the end, remains immature, refusing to accept his punishment; but God still shows him mercy.

What does Cain teach us about the psychology of sin?

Does the Bible make us keepers of one another?

Explain the image of the blood shed in murder calling forth the curse of the land.

4

Preservation

Genesis 9:8–17

The mercy that God shows to Cain aims at protecting Cain's life. Just as God punished Adam and Eve for their wrongdoing yet clothed their nakedness and provided for their future, so God punishes Cain's murder of Abel without writing Cain off completely. This characteristic of the Old Testament God is overlooked by those who seek vengeance to the point of annihilation. It is overlooked by the Bible itself in its most objectionable passages, where it supports holy warfare and extermination of the enemy. Today some of the worst offenders against the example of the biblical God are the Muslim terrorists who murder in the name of their territorial grievances, but unfortunately the Christian Crusaders and Puritan armies were all too like them. If the Yahwist God can render very thorough justice and punishment and yet continue to care for even the most sinful creatures, it would seem to follow that the best of today's peacemakers and servants of justice should develop a similar capacity, never failing to call a spade a spade while not forgetting that every sinner deserves kindness.

The story of primeval humanity that we find in the first eleven chapters of Genesis only further declines after Cain. By the time of Noah humanity is so wicked that God decides to flood the earth with destruction. The passage we now consider concerns the covenant God makes with Noah after the flood and helps us recall the beautiful sign of the rainbow. God has blessed Noah, who functions as a second Adam (a second start for the human race), and has urged him, like Adam and Eve, to be fruitful. God has given Noah dominion over the earth and even the right to eat animal flesh. Now God is concerned to assure Noah and his children that the destruction visited by the flood will never be repeated. God makes a covenant with Noah promising that all of creation will be preserved from destruction. The rainbow will serve as the sign of this covenant, as though to remind God of the pledge. When we remember that ancient peoples often thought of the rainbow as the weapon from which God shot the arrows of heavenly lightning, we realize that this sign implied that God had put away this instrument of wrath in token of the pledge to preserve the earth.

The Noachite covenant, as it is sometimes called, was considered to apply to all human beings. Whereas the pacts with Abraham, Moses, and David bore only on Israel, the pact with Noah was universal. In biblical interpretation, therefore, all the nations and all subhuman creation has a great dignity, for God has pledged to preserve both humanity and creation. If either perishes, the fault will not lie with God. Only in our own time has it become possible to contemplate seriously the annihilation of humanity and all of earthly life. Only in our own time, therefore, have theologians and other reflective people had to question the commitment to preserving life that both the Bible and the incredible complexity of the interactions that make life possible testify God has always had.

When genocides are attempted, as they have been many times in human history, not the least of them in our own century, the people concerned certainly are bound to question God's care for them. Most of the people who have been threatened with extinction have felt themselves bonded to a Supreme Being, and all of them have wondered how such a God could allow their destruction. Indeed, the special poignancy and edge in discussions of the Holocaust of the Jews in the Nazi death camps is the sense of election that Jews traditionally have had. Thinking themselves God's chosen people, they have had to wonder all the more about the divine justice. To be sure, their predecessors at such times as the exile to Babylon (586 B.C.E.), the destruction of the Temple and Jerusalem by the Romans (70 C.E.), and the repulsion from the Iberian Peninsula (1492 C.E.) chased similar thoughts. The more intimately one depicts the divine favor and promise of love, the greater problem one has with divine providence and justice when massive sufferings arise.

The Noachite covenant suggests a broader framework within which our sense of the divine justice can expand. God promises each individual sufficient grace to make that person's existence a good thing rather than a pernicious cruelty. Somehow, believers in the biblical God have reasoned, God will recompense the faithful for their sufferings and wipe every tear from their eyes. God also promises creation sufficient joy, peace, and success to justify having made it. Otherwise, God is a perverse creator, a heavenly sadist. Both the subjects of the Noachite covenant (all of humanity and all of creation) and the subjects of the Israelite and Christian covenants (Jews and Christians) to date have survived. To date, therefore, God has kept the divine side of the bargain, however much we may still feel minded to assault heaven for the sufferings that millions of human beings, among them Jews and Christians, and other creatures have undergone. Nowadays, though, every sort of covenant stands under the cloud of nuclear winter. Nowadays, only the other planets and the other galaxies seem secure. To be sure, this means that much more than 99 and 44/100 percent of creation sings the divine praises. But we want to know that the specifically human part, the part that Genesis singles out as being God's very image, also will survive.

I think there is no way that theologians, any more than scientists or politicians, can assure their readers that the earth will avoid nuclear holocaust. The covenant made with Noah can stand for the many symbols and assurances of biblical religion that God certainly is on the side of being and life rather than nothingness and death. This implies that nuclear holocaust would completely violate God's will. But we cannot take the covenant made with Noah, or any other expression of biblical faith, so literally that we think we can know exactly what the divine mystery will or will not allow to happen. If we think that God truly has made humanity, images of God, responsible for earthly creation, we have to accept the real possibility that, like Cain, humanity will fail to accept its responsibility and will flee to murderous immaturity.

What mature partners to a covenant with God should do in this situation can, of course, be debated, but I think they should be signal witnesses to several judgments whose embrace could radically contest the nations' rush toward war. First, people who firmly believe in the oneness of the biblical God so that no other treasure strongly competes with God in their hearts should be able to announce in clear voices and exemplary lives that virtually nothing could ever justify imperiling earthly creation through nuclear warfare. Certainly, to risk nuclear warfare for the sake of maintaining its high standard of living or its supposed prestige in the world would brand a nation utterly atheistic. Indeed, even to risk nuclear war for the sake of maintaining one's form of government and one's treasured set of personal freedoms would be to blaspheme against the Creator and violate biblical common sense. Nothing in the biblical covenants says that democracy, let alone Marxism, has God's approval as the sole form of government compatible with the intent of creation.

Second, from this bottom line comes a further implication for people of biblical faith: the need for any form of government or any political power in the world to bring itself into line with the current facts about the dangers of nuclear energy and so shift to policies that further distance it and its interactions with other political powers from the brink of conflict or meltdown. Not to be moving toward a day when there are no nuclear bombs, no risky nuclear power plants, no murderous hatreds among peoples, and no contrasts in standards of living sufficient to provoke war would be seen as a violation of the Noachite pact.

What does the use of the rainbow suggest about the imagination of the biblical authors?

What have been the main horrors of the chosen people?

How should monotheism slow a people's rush to war?

5

Justice

Exodus 23:1–8

When Israel thought about the Mosaic covenant, which was the most influential version of the bond struck between the people and God, it spent much time and energy pondering the sort of conduct that the privilege of being God's chosen people entailed. The laws for worship that we find in the Hebrew Bible testify to the holiness the people felt was incumbent upon them if they were to come into the presence of the holy God and not be destroyed. Similarly, the many laws that we find about social relations rely for their deepest rationale on Israel's feeling that it had to be righteous and just if it were to live as its election by God implied.

The laws that we find in the first verses of Exodus 23 generally are taken by scholars to be part of the "Covenant Code." This code comes after the Ten Commandments (Ex. 20:1–17) and specifies rather miscellaneous obligations—ways that the covenantal relationship with God ought to work out in daily life. Although some of the legal materials in the Bible probably go back to the patriarchal period, when the earliest Israelites observed the sort of tribal ethics typical of the nomadic peoples of the ancient Near East, biblical tradition tends to cluster the laws that arose at the establishment of the people during and after the exodus from Egypt around the person of Moses. The conceit is that God gave to Moses on Mount Sinai all of the regulations that came to have customary force in Israel. Historical critics tend to regard the laws of this Covenant Code as reflecting a time after the conquest of the promised land, when the tribes enjoyed a somewhat settled agricultural existence. The literary editing responsible for the code could be as late as 725 B.C.E., since it seems to occur in the midst of materials that fuse the Yahwist stratum with other layers of tradition only organized by the mid-eighth century.

For our purposes, these verses exemplify the high standard of justice and probity that the Bible thought followed upon proper relationship to God. At the least, we may examine them with the possibility in mind that, if any society were in fact to observe them, it would enjoy a level of fair-dealing that would make it a light to the Gentiles and a winning testimony to the true God. Notice, for instance, the simple demand of verse 1: no lying. The rabbis would take a law such as this, consider it in the context of the whole of the Torah, and suggest that it should penetrate many different layers of social behavior and individual conscience. At the level where it had inspired behavior truly worthy of God, it would mean that all distortion of the truth—misinformation, mental reservation, stonewalling, tricky small print in the contract, and the like—would be abhorred as violating the Lord's demand that the covenanted people deal only in the coin of truth.

As if to exemplify this deeper and more generalized implication, the second injunction of verse 1 forbids joining the wicked and supporting their wrongful suits with slanted testimony. If we took this injunction deeply to heart, we probably would think that our present legal system in the United States, for all its virtues, falls seriously short of what the covenant requires. Indeed, we probably would think that our central assumptions about the rights of all people, even the guilty, to vigorous defense and advocacy require considerable criticism. I must question whether one can, in fact, be a full servant of the God of the covenant and practice law impartially, leaving all judgments of innocence and guilt to judges and juries. Can one be equally ready and willing to argue either side of a case or defend either party?

Verse 2 also suggests that the biblical fusion of ethics and law is tighter than our own. It insists that each person is responsible for avoiding evil, even if a whole crowd is marching to accomplish it. No witness should be given that is not fully honest, even if a multitude are ready and willing to speak up prejudicially. Verse 3 even demands that witnesses make certain they are not partial to the poor and, by implication, prejudiced against the wealthy. All the more, one suspects, we are not to be partial to the rich and prejudiced against the poor. Rather, in all cases our only partiality is to be for the truth and our only prejudice against dishonesty. We could not ask for a more demanding public stance and citizenship than that. If such radical, thoroughgoing honesty were to visit any people, its justice would be a wonder comparable to the midnight sun.

Verses 4–5 take us to the demanding area of treatment of our enemies. They are a good verification of the Jewish claim that much in the ethics of Jesus had strong biblical and rabbinic precedent, for here is a concrete specification of Jesus' command in the Sermon on the Mount (Matt. 5:44) that we must love our enemies and do good to those who persecute us. We are to deal with the animals (and, presumably, all the other goods) of our enemy as we would deal with the animals belonging to our friends or to members of our own families. Part of the reason, no doubt, is the biblical sense that animals, too, come from the living God and deserve good treatment. But another reason is that biblical justice deliberately transcends the tendentiousness and particularism of a tribal sense of righteousness. For the tribe, frequently, anything that a member of the extended family does among outsiders has to be defended, and any misfortune that befalls an enemy is cause for joy. The Bible would force all of its readers to mount above this tribal level and reject its emotional satisfactions (the dramatic life of always feeling something strongly and not caring greatly whether the feeling be love or hate). It would have us exhibit the responsibility of being made in God's image and so called to do good for its own sake, simply because it is right and just.

Verse 6 balances verse 3, making sure that we not show prejudice against the poor and deny them their justice. Verse 7 is a warning, reminiscent of the maxims we find in the later wisdom literature, to stay far from lying and those who bring false charges. The idea is that, if we want to be truthful and honest as the holiness of God requires, we must not consort with liars or tour the province of false speech. Note in this verse as well the explicit promise that God will punish the wicked—those who slay the innocent and the righteous. However much we want to update the notion of divine judgment so that it avoids the distortions of the popular imagery of devils and hellfire, we cannot deny that the Bible promises sanctions for what we do—reward for doing good and appropriate punishment for doing evil. It will not abide any vacuum of justice that would justify our thinking human existence a game so tilted that only fools follow the rules.

The last of our prosaic laws, which forbids taking bribes, hints at what the Bible takes to be God's stake in the entire matter of legal justice and general fair-dealing. The Bible equates God's stake with the cause of those who are in the right. As the Johannine literature of the New Testament will equate God with light and admit no moral darkness into the divine nature, so the Code of the Covenant insists that "God" and "the right" coincide. To be sure, God is the large entity, and we have finally to submit our human notions of righteousness to the divine mystery. But a very important affirmation remains: God is the champion of what human beings know in pure conscience is right and just. Conversely, God is the enemy of what human beings know in pure conscience is wrong and unjust.

Everyone who serves and abets genuine justice is a friend of God, a person worthy of the covenant. Everyone who perverts justice—who lies, cheats, delays, defrauds—is an enemy of God and a person unworthy of the covenant. And the justice at issue here is not, of course, the mere letter of the law—even of the good law, let alone the law that has been cast prejudicially, warped by special interests, from the beginning. The justice at issue here is simple, elementary honesty and fairness. God abhors the lies and slants that create at least half of any society's pain and rage.

How does Exodus fuse ethics and law?

What are the main drawbacks to tribal justice?

Can one without qualification make God the enemy of what human beings know in pure conscience is wrong and unjust?

6

Holiness

Leviticus 18:30–19:5

Many treatments of peacemaking and working for justice neglect the specifically religious dimension revealed by worship. For secular people committed to peace and justice, it can seem enough to try to rectify present unfairnesses and prepare for the day when human beings will cooperate rather than fight. The biblical sense of peace and justice takes this praiseworthy attitude to a higher level. For the Bible, the God who defines what human nature most intimately is and how human prosperity is best realized above all is holy. This God must be worshiped in spirit and truth, and such worship is the training ground, the site of the formation, that can make peacemaking a matter of what one is rather than just a matter of what one chooses to work on.

We must admit, of course, that the cult described in the Bible has its problems, not the least of which is a tendency to hone the people to intolerance. The exclusiveness that Israel linked with pure cult could easily prove a barrier to peaceful negotiations with its neighbors, while the linking of total victory, to the point of wholesale slaughter, with the purity required of adherents of the holy God calls zealous worship deeply into question.

My interpretation of the biblical call to holiness and worship, therefore, is clearly that—my own interpretation. I see holiness as necessarily an ally of justice and peace, because to my mind the biblical God is holy precisely in ways that encourage the people of the covenant to labor for what is right and build up what makes for the tranquillity of good order. Conversely, I find interpretations of the holiness of God that lead to zealotry, fanaticism, separatism, and hatred of one's enemies distortions of the overall theology of the Bible. I believe that when the classical prophets called for mercy rather than sacrifice, for justice rather than ritualistic punctiliousness, they made a similar judgment.

Leviticus is the book of the Torah that most fully details how ancient Israel thought about the fusion of God, cult, and holiness. Chapters 17–26 are commonly called the "Holiness Code," and scholars tend to consider them a unit of tradition associated with the priestly stratum but probably assembled somewhat before that stratum had been fully organized. If we place the organization of P around 500 B.C.E., the Holiness Code might be as much as 125 years older.

Our text begins with a warning against defilements (through sexual irregularities) that have previously been described. The consequence of such defilements has been described as being vomited out of the land (the sort of conviction we found when we considered the consequences of Cain's murder of Abel) and being cut off from the (chosen) people. Ancient Israel thought of sexuality as the mechanism for the transmission of life, God's direct gift. To engage in sexual practices that endangered the proper transmission of life was deeply abhorrent, so the penalties attached were extremely heavy. Indeed, sinners of any serious sort were considered "defiled," as though dirt or pitch had smeared them. They could not come into contact with the holy God, because the conflict between their filth and God's purity would endanger the entire tribe. Like electricity reacting to a damaged carrier, the holiness of God would explode on contact with people who dared to approach it with unclean hearts or hands.

Verse 2 announces the leitmotiv: "You shall be holy; for I the Lord your God am holy." Note, though, how quickly and naturally holiness is translated into social practice as well as cultic purity. Reverence shown toward one's parents, for instance, expresses the holiness required of the people chosen by the holy God. So does keeping the Sabbath a day of rest and worship. Both of these requirements were enshrined in the Ten Commandments, and so both were pegs on which Jewish tradition hung considerable social ethics.

The reverence due one's parents was more than showing proper gratitude for the source of one's life and proper awe at the miracle of life itself. It was also a practical way of keeping order in the family and a practical way of assuring that those with the greater experience would have the greater say.

The maintenance of the Sabbath was primarily a matter of confessing the sole sovereignty of the one God, but it was also a way of reaffirming the solidarity of all the members of the community by assembling all in common worship. At such worship the God that all adored would again be praised, and the divine laws to which all were bound again would ring out imperatively. A people gaining domestic order and communal identity through its obedience to its God would be a people in good shape.

Verse 4 deals with idolatry, the Bible's summary symbol for false worship and false theology. We can exaggerate the degree to which the Israelites in fact dealt with their God as a pure mystery (the very force of the polemic against idolatry that runs through both the Law and the Prophets suggests that it was a deep and persistent problem), but there is no denying that many key passages in the Bible proclaim an unqualified monotheism. The gods of the neighboring nations are mocked as worthless products of human hands, while the fertility rites that meant so much to ancient peoples deeply immersed in the cycles of nature are abhorred as both a distortion of sexuality and a lack of trust in the true source of nature's prosperity.

At the core of Israelite faith was the intuition, discernible from as early as the call of Abraham, that a single holy source was responsible for the world and, amazingly, desired to have particular ties with this given people. Holiness and the social ethics that it inspired rooted in such a monotheistic impulse. To disperse the divine power and goodness among a plethora of natural forces was, to the mind of the most influential biblical theologians, an error so fundamental that it had to root in bad will and corruption of heart.

The last of our verses, verse 5, deals with the sacrifice for peace offerings. In the context of Levitical thought, this was a special kind of sacrifice associated with eating a meal. Leviticus 3 and 7 detail the animal to be sacrificed and the various subspecies of the prayers. For example, the thank offering was appropriate on such occasions as release from prison and recovery from serious illness (see Psalm 107). I am more interested, however, in the general tenor of the verse, which is that when one wants to approach God so as to augment peace (good relations both with God and within the community) one must take care to approach properly. For the Levitical legislators such a proper approach implied specific matters: cleansings, kind of animal parts dealt with, times at which to eat, and so on. For Christian heirs of Leviticus the point rather would seem to be the dispositions of love of God and love of neighbor that Jesus made the foundation of his social ethics.

If we are to be holy on the model of Jesus, our hearts must be open to only one treasure. It is the love of God poured forth in our hearts by the Holy Spirit (Rom. 5:5) that makes us pleasing to God and gives us the divine peace. Similarly, it is the love of God that can cause us to treat well even the enemies that persecute us, for the Spirit can remind us that God makes the rain to fall and the sun to shine on just and unjust alike (see Matt. 5:43–46). The love of God is the source of the peace that the children of God spontaneously long to make. Like justice—basic honesty and fair-dealing—it is less a matter of choices we make or goals we target than a matter of something we express and intend in all of our actions. If we are filled with the love of God through the Spirit who makes us cry, "Abba, Father," we are bound to want creativity and peace rather than war and destruction. As well, our actions are bound to tend toward peace rather than war. This is the nature of the love, the life, ruling our hearts, the center of our selves. So, too, our actions are bound to express the light of God, the divine honesty and justice. The Spirit no more can lie or defraud than light can coexist with darkness. If we are holy, we will be just.

What light does the call to holiness shed on the laws of Leviticus?

What should be the relationship between cult and social justice?

What are the problems in the Levitical stress on purity?

7

Jubilee

Leviticus 25:8–14

A high point of the Holiness Code is the treatment of the Jubilee year in Leviticus 25. The assumption that works throughout the chapter, but which is made explicit only in verse 23, is that the land belongs to God. Thus the land is to participate in Israel's enjoyment of a sabbath by lying fallow every seventh year (25:1–7), and the people are to celebrate a grand sabbatical year, a sabbath of sabbaths, every fiftieth year. At that time things shall revert to the ideal state they can be imagined to have had at God's beginning, and abusive situations that have developed shall be righted. Verse 10, for example, forsees the release of all captives, indentured servants, and slaves (liberty for all inhabitants of the land). Families shall return to their ancestral landholdings, with the stipulation that sales and leases through which the original holders have alienated their land shall be fairly compensated.

Let us reflect briefly on these two prescriptions for the Jubilee year—granting liberty to all the inhabitants of the land and returning holdings to their original owners—and then deal with the utopian imagination that the Bible displays here and in many other places.

It is not clear that Israel ever actually celebrated a Jubilee year as Leviticus 25 enjoins, but through the legislation described in this chapter it did make plain its sense of how things ought to be at the best of times, when both the people and the land were enjoying God's rest. First, there ought to be liberty for all and enslavement for none. The Bible did not require a sweeping reform of all wrongheaded social customs such as slavery. We find slavery accepted in the Old Testament just as we find it accepted by the apostle Paul. But both the Old Testament and Paul not only mitigated the abuses to which slaves were liable but also spoke of an ideal situation in which the land would offer liberty to all or the Body of Christ would know neither slave nor free (Gal. 3:28). Slavery and the other species of a lack of liberty, therefore, were sensed to be much less than what ought to obtain when God was in heaven and all was right with the world. By legislating a return to this state of freedom every fifty years, Leviticus wanted to offer Israel a way of imagining a regular return to ideal conditions and making a fresh start.

The same applies to the legislation for returning land to its original possessors and overturning the alienations that had occurred through renting or sale. This legislation suggested a mechanism for keeping people close to their land and so mindful of how the land was God's gift to them. It was meant to offset the profiteering, speculation, and other sorts of manipulation that tended to make the land serve only the greedy and ambitious. Because the land finally belonged to God, God could order its regular redistribution into holdings that provided the people stability and a good living.

Leviticus 25 is one of the clearest indications we have that the Bible never thought in terms of what we today mean by private property. For the Bible property, land, and the earth and its fruits exist for the common good. People may have traditional associations with particular parcels, and so certain rights thereon, but the more basic judgment of the Bible is that the goods of the earth exist for all of the earth's people. The Creator did not make the world for the flourishing of a few energetic entrepreneurs, let alone a few multinational conglomerates. The Jubilee legislation of Leviticus suggests that God gave the land itself rights to rest and proper treatment and that God further considered the land to be a trust. Human beings were to administer this trust fairly, so that no one waxed fat with luxuries while others lacked necessities.

The people who are working for land reform in the midwestern United States are trying to revive some of these biblical convictions. Horrified by the pollution of the land that recent development has brought and horrified even more by the plight of the nation's farmers, they have gone back to their biblical roots and realized that free enterprise on the model of recent conglomerate farming operations and real estate developments strongly conflicts with biblical teaching. In the Bible, the plight of all the people is the first matter of concern, and the state of the land itself is a close second. If the land is used in ways that bring significant numbers of citizens into poverty, neglect, and despair, such use must be condemned. The fact that powerful interests can legally manipulate the land and create such suffering does not carry much weight. The Bible would simply say that legality of this sort has no ultimate credentials. The law of God is far more important than the skewed codes of sinful people.

In any genuine conflict, believers must obey God rather than human authorities (Acts 5:29). This does not mean that those working for land reform should immediately run out and disobey the laws of their state on property taxes, zoning restrictions, farm foreclosures, and the like. It does mean that those working for land reform should find in the churches and the synagogues solid allies in their efforts both to return the land to the service of the common good and to dispute, decry, and discredit the selfishness which now so often parades under the banner of development and entrepreneurship.

A utopia is a no-place. It is a realm of imagination where things are as conscience and faith declare they ought to be. Indeed, faith declares that justice and peace, for the land and all other aspects of creation, obtain right now in God's view of and God's judgments on the way things are. Thinking about the implications of the radical monotheism of biblical religion, ethicists easily can conclude that God merely tolerates our wars and injustices for the sake of the freedom we human beings need if we are to love God and one another genuinely. Genuine love cannot be compelled or constrained. It must come from a personal appreciation of the goodness of the beloved and flow forth as an expression of our whole mind, heart, soul, and strength. This love is so precious in God's sight that to secure its necessary conditions God puts up with the abuses of creation that human freedom can generate. God can save human beings from their sins and for divine life only through free exchanges of love. But God certainly can and has structured human freedom and its relation to the physical world in such a way that the freer we become and the more capable of loving in ways that are salvific the more we will see that the goods of the earth are for all of the earth's people.

This sort of theological reasoning is utopian in the sense that no place on earth fully incarnates it. If we castigate the contemporary United States as a place where neither the land nor our fellow human beings are treated as the love of God requires, we have also to castigate all other times and places throughout history. We must temper our utopian convictions, therefore, and join God in putting up with human imperfections. On the other hand, we must also try to appreciate the depth of the justice and peace for the land that biblical passages such as Leviticus 25 suggest God desires. The Jubilee ultimately is more indicative of how things stand in the sight of God than are forty-nine years of business as usual. The Jubilee is the rejoicing that comes from God when liberty prevails in the land and no one gouges.

Why does Leviticus not sanction private property?

What is the main intent of the symbolism of the Jubilee year?

What does a serious but not literal reading of Leviticus 25 suggest for present-day reform of land usage?

8

Hearing and Teaching

Deuteronomy 6:4–9

Most biblical scholars today consider the Book of Deuteronomy to come from a stratum of tradition different from those we have seen in the Torah thus far. And while one may speak of a proto-Deuteronomic tradition that used materials from a period shortly after the United Kingdom of Solomon and of an early consolidation of this tradition (which later included materials we now find in the Former Prophets—the books of Joshua, Judges, Samuel, and Kings) by 800 B.C.E., the final version of Deuteronomy probably was reached only around 400 B.C.E., when it was separated from the "Deuteronomistic history" (the larger tradition that included the materials now found in the Former Prophets) and joined with Genesis, Exodus, Leviticus, and Numbers to make the Torah—the five books of Moses that Jews have always considered the innermost core of divine instruction.

The basic theme of the Deuteronomic theology is that, if Israel will keep to the laws of the covenant that God struck with it through Moses on Mount Sinai, then Israel will prosper. If Israel fails to keep these laws, it will suffer dire misfortunes. We do well to remember that by 400 B.C.E. the biblical theologians could look back on five centuries laden with disasters. From the divisions of the United Kingdom at the death of Solomon around 921 to the fall of the Northern Kingdom in 721 to Assyria and the fall of the Southern Kingdom in 586 to Babylon, reams of suffering begged explanation. The explanation fashioned by the Deuteronomistic historians was that Israel's punishments were due to its sins, above all its sin of idolatry. Our present text, Deuteronomy 6:4–9, is a classic statement of this theology in positive form. Indeed, known as the Shema ("hear"), it is the most popular and hallowed expression of Jewish monotheism. The mezuzah that one finds on the door of traditional Jewish homes contains the Shema (and also Deuteronomy 11:13–21), as do the phylacteries (*tefillin*) worn on the left arm and forehead by Orthodox Jewish men. It is apparent that these were considered verses whose regular recall would keep believers centered as God wished them to be.

What is it that Israel, old and new, is to hear? That the Lord our God is one—unique, without rival, the sole possessor of divinity in the exact sense. Also, that we are to love God exhaustively, as we love no one and nothing else. The Shema makes a claim upon its hearers that is exclusive and comprehensive. To its mind there is only one center to human existence, only one ordering of human affairs that squares with the truth. If people fit themselves to the order that the sole God gives, they will walk in the truth and enjoy all the benefits of the light that truth sheds. If people miss this order through deafness to the Lord's call, they will wander in darkness and reap self-ruin. The basic issue could not be presented more clearly or starkly.

The rest of the verses deal with how to keep the love of God alive in people's hearts and dominant in people's minds. First, parents are to teach this diligently (the root meaning of *diligent* is "loving") to their children. We could gloss this first consequence by saying that when mothers and fathers do make the love of God the cornerstone of how they raise their children they obey the first commandment in the biblical handbook for parenting. Children taught that the great romance of their lives is the love affair they have with the beauty that moves the stars and the goodness that gives all life its breath are given a treasure that cannot fail. Parents whose own sense of life is that it comes down from a "Father of lights" (James 1:17) as a series of good gifts are handing on the one thing necessary.

The mystery of God that beckons in everything that raises the human spirit holds out a freedom, as well as a peace, that the world cannot give. Responding to such beckoning, a child will never be the captive of mammon, the pawn of advertising, the dupe of jingoism or ideology. The mystery of God that is challenged by every appearance of evil, every slash at the human spirit, is similarly primordial and thus useful. Mammon, glittery pleasure, and secular causes so obviously fail the challenge flung down by evil that the silence and darkness of a truly mysterious God, a God whose Son might freely suffer for the sins of the world, become credible and thus genuinely comforting.

Second, the other ways of keeping the primacy of the divine love (God's love for human beings, as well as human beings' love for God) vital prominently include theological discussion and artistic stimuli. If people love God they will love theology—not the academic discipline but the amateur (the loving) search of faith to understand the wonders of its God. If people love God, they will speak of God, sing of God, and adorn their homes and their places of worship with beautiful stimuli.

Israel loved discussions of Torah. Judaism has always been a highly verbal, articulate, argumentative religious tradition. And even though Israelite monotheism was interpreted as putting a brake on representations of God, and so on religious art, lest the uniqueness of God be distorted and idolatry feel encouraged, Christian monotheism, structured by the incarnation of God's word, has felt free to develop sounds and sights into sacraments, performative artworks of faith.

True enough, biblical monotheism has served as a basis for criticizing Christian worship and devotional life when they seemed to get lost among the icons and forget the singularity of the divine mystery. But the other side of the story of the Christian response to the Shema, the Christian interpretation of how to make the love of God and theology alive, has been a license to follow the Johannine Christ in confecting "signs"—material forms through which people might learn what God is like in human terms, how the love of God might look and sound and feel.

The bearing of the biblical call to a lively monotheistic faith on work for peace and justice is not hard to indicate. If the love of God really is the first passion in people's hearts, most of the disordered passions that produce war and injustice have no ground in which to grow. Certainly the virulent growth of money, power, and prestige is greatly reduced so that people feel little temptation to pivot life around them. Certainly it becomes much more possible to believe that the goods of the earth exist for all of the earth's people and that the responsibility of the images of God is to share these goods fairly. And it even becomes possible to temper one's thirst for vengeance, one's hunger to answer each tit with a tat, because compared to God the dispossessions we suffer and the slights that slash us are bound to seem second-rate matters. Widespread poverty and suffering of course remain gross evils crying out to God for redress, but widespread poverty and suffering are far from the only matters on the agenda of the generals, politicians, and industrialists who play such major roles in present-day warmaking.

The Shema implies that the earth is the Lord's and the fullness thereof. It implies that true human prosperity will come through the worship, responsible parenting, creative work, relief of suffering, and nurture of hungry minds, carved out for and through God by us, our saints and our wise. Granted adequate food, housing, and bodily health, human prosperity is mainly a matter of mind and spirit. Basic research, beautiful music, and elevating art require relatively little monetary expenditure. The implication of the worldwide crises that we now suffer—in the ecosphere, the international economy, the global sense of purpose—is that we will not survive and prosper unless the five billion of us shift away from the consumerist, militant, egocentric blindness that dominates the Northern nations and tempts the Southern nations. We shall survive to the year 2200 and prosper in a substantial sense by following counsel such as that of Deuteronomy 6—by worshiping a real and thus mysterious God, making the education of our children to spiritual maturity our first responsibility, and developing cultures whose talk and adornment flow primarily from love of God toward peace and justice on earth.

How would you explain to a teenager what the Shema would have us hear?

How can religious art serve the intents of the Shema?

How is a life filled with the love of God freed from many of the causes of war and injustice?

9

Destruction and Love

Deuteronomy 7:1–9

In this text the Deuteronomic theology combines some of its worst features with some of its best. Let us first reflect on the several striking features of the text itself and then ask what they suggest about reconceiving the status of foreigners.

The text begins with a reference to the Lord's gift of the holy land to be conquered by the forces led by Joshua (the literary time of the text is a speech of Moses prior to this conquest). God is assumed to be the first of Israel's warriors, the champion responsible for all of its victories. Into the mouth of the holy God is placed the commandment to destroy those who had possessed the holy land (Canaan) utterly. The reason given is that making pacts with such foreigners, showing them mercy, and practicing intermarriage with them would turn Israel away from its God and so rouse God's anger to destroy it. Therefore the foreign people themselves and all of their religious artifacts are to be completely destroyed.

At the time that the Torah became "scripture" (writing canonized as regulative for faith) for Israel, about 400 B.C.E., the reforms of Ezra and Nehemiah that we read about in the books that go under their names were in full flower. Israel had been at the work of restoring itself after the fifty horrible years of exile in Babylon for some time, and the realization had grown that such a restoration required more than rebuilding the Temple and reestablishing a proper cult. The reformers thought that Israel was in danger of drowning in the pagan cultures of its surrounding neighbors, so they legislated a strict segregation, an apartheid, that they hoped would keep their fellow Jews ethnically and religiously pure.

It seems probable that the destructive separatism enjoined by our text reflects these postexilic reforms. That certainly does not justify the evil latent in the injunctions to destroy the Canaanite enemies, but it does somewhat explain them. For the sake of what they thought was necessary to preserve their people, the authors and editors pressed the holiness of the Mosaic God out of shape and tried to make their own obligations to be holy a justification for despising foreigners to the point of slaughter.

Verse 6 carries such a justification: Israel is a people holy to God, chosen by God out of all the peoples of the earth to be God's special possession. Once again, we must try to imagine a situation of cultural crisis and hear in this verse the efforts of those who were desperately trying to save Israel to provide a rationale for Jewish separateness. Unfortunately, the notion of special election is only slightly less objectionable than the notion of holy warfare with which it has often been allied.

Precisely how either Jews or Christians ought to understand their chosenness by God or the uniqueness of the self-disclosures of God to them is a complicated theological problem. On the one hand, neither group can deny its conviction that what God has done for it, what God has made available in the world through it, is distinctive, indeed unique, and of truly unsurpassable significance. On the other hand, both groups will find in their history, if they face it squarely, too many times when this conviction has made them arrogant, misanthropic, separatist, and terribly destructive. Because Christians have had far greater population and power throughout the past twenty centuries (today there are nearly seventy-five Christians for every Jew), the Christian sense of chosenness (along with Christian anti–Semitism) has done by far the greater damage. However, both faiths have given foreigners good reason to think that the God of the Bible is unacceptably partisan. Indeed, at times foreigners have had good reason to think the God of the Bible a bloodthirsty warmonger.

Verses 7–8, to be sure, offer good reasons why "chosenness" should never have become a matter for pride or boasting. The Deuteronomists knew that what they enjoyed through the covenant was purely a matter of divine grace. If they did not think this as a result of theological inference—a God who is a genuine creator and savior always has the primacy—they thought it as a result of simple observation of Israelite history. Again and again Israel failed the lofty standards of the covenant and showed that God certainly had not chosen it because of its worthiness. (The text shies away from this matter of worthiness judged by behavior, preferring to deal with the less embarrassing matter of numerical size.) Only the divine love itself could explain the covenant and all of its attendant gifts. Only God could explain the goodness of God.

The case is the same for Christians, of course. Nothing in the church explains why God should have made it a conduit of the saving divine love. Nothing in the moral stature of the first companions of Jesus explained why they were blessed with discipleship, and nothing in the moral stature of later Christians has explained why they should have been blessed to hear Jesus call them not servants but friends. All of the priority, the grace, the explanation lies on God's side. On the human side there is no cause at all for boasting.

A truly humble train of biblical religionists certainly would remove much of the scandal in the notion of chosenness, election, or special covenant, but it would not remove it entirely. Jews have further shaved down the scandal of chosenness by reflecting that they received the covenant for the sake of the Gentile nations, whom they were to serve as a light of example, as well as for themselves. Christians have thought similarly, and one finds in the New Testament itself assurances that the grace of God works in all people of good will (see, for instance, Acts 10:34). But this impulse toward generosity (if we may give any human tendency to pass judgment on how God distributes love and favor a good name) has often been in tension with, indeed has often been overpowered by, a strain of Christian conviction that only explicit believers in the name of Jesus could be saved. Seeming warrants for this point of view included Acts 4:12 and John 3:18. The time has come—indeed, it has long been at hand—to make it plain that any group claiming an exclusive patent on the mechanisms of salvation is an idolatrous menace. The God who brought Israel out of Egypt with a mighty hand and brought Jesus out of the jaws of death for the sake of a new creation desires the salvation of all people (1 Tim. 2:4).

The best verse in our text, therefore, is the last: "Know therefore that the Lord your God is God, the faithful God who keeps covenant and steadfast love with those who love him and keep his commandments, to a thousand generations." We need only interpret this description of God as applying worldwide to have the theological foundations necessary for peacemaking and global justice.

The text assures us that God truly is God—mysterious, sovereign and certainly no divinity that we can put in our pocket or get to underwrite our wars. It assures us that God is faithful; the fault is not with God but with ourselves. God stands by all who stand by God—all who follow the Spirit moving in their hearts and show the signs of the Spirit in their lives. The summary signs of fidelity to the divine Spirit are radical honesty and love. Wherever we come across people who do what is right and build up faith and hope, we come across people moved by the Spirit of God. The names such people call themselves matter far less than the lives such people lead. If they want to explain their lives in terms of allegiance to Buddha or Marx or simple honesty, that is their right. God alone descries their hearts and passes adequate judgment on their allegiances. Sufficient for us is what people do.

Jesus promulgated this criterion when he said we could know people by their fruits (see Matt. 7:20). The international conventions we need if we are to save the world from holocaust and establish economic justice are matters of fruits. Doctrines and creeds, however precious, are secondary. As Matthew 25 shows, Jesus was more interested in deeds.

Can one say that the command to destroy Israel's Canaanite enemies utterly was an evil, ungodly injunction?

How has the biblical notion of chosenness contributed to

slaughter and suffering by Jews, and even more by Christians and Muslims?

Can the notion of chosenness be redeemed by seeing the chosenness as a primacy in service?

10

Life and Death

Deuteronomy 30:15–20

Toward the end of Moses' long speech, before the final section of the book that deals with the death of the great lawgiver, we find a rhetorical summation. The commandments of the covenant having been laid out, the authors want to move their readers to embrace what has been prescribed. This entails showing that the Torah, conceived as an ethics of performance, is practical and brings unparalleled benefits. The translation for ourselves might be that the instruction of the biblical God shows us why and how working for peace and justice will reward us.

Deuteronomy 30 as a whole is remarkably upbeat. The opening verses promise that obedience will bring Israel the restoration of its fortunes (recall again the postexilic situation in which the book was canonized), God's compassion, and the regathering of a people that had been scattered. Restored to the land, Israel will feel God purify its heart so that it can do what the Shema enjoins (verse 6). Obedience will lead to such further benefits as the cursing of Israel's enemies and the prospering of Israel in children, land, and animals.

Verses 11–14 make it explicit that the Torah is not something hard or far off: "The word is very near you; it is in your mouth and in your heart, so that you can do it." Traditional Judaism took this last verse seriously and taught itself to think of the Torah as a joy. The view of the Law that Christians find in the New Testament therefore can be deceptive. While certainly any code with 613 different prescriptions would run the risk of legalism, the joy in hearing and doing God's word that the rabbis experienced kept many, if not most, of them and their people from the narrowness that "pharisaism" connotes. Indeed, as recent scholarship has stressed, the Pharisees on the whole had a wonderful appreciation of the wholeness that the Torah ought to bring people.

The verses of our chosen text bring this positive movement of chapter 30 to a climax. Moses comes to his peroration by making a clear contrast between the way of obedience to Torah and the way of disobedience. One gives life and the other gives death. This is the bias of Deuteronomic theology, as we mentioned previously. With less nuance than what we find in other parts of the Bible, Deuteronomic theology is willing to equate obedience to Torah with prospering in quite historical and material terms. Equally, it is willing to equate disobedience with disaster. The Book of Job suggests the crisis that had befallen Deuteronomic theology by 90 C.E., when Job and the other Writings were accepted as the third group of canonical writings. At that time (Jerusalem had been destroyed in 70 C.E.) it was less clear that one could equate historical disasters with religious failings. Indeed, Luke 13:1–5 (edited about the same time) seems to make Jesus explicitly repudiate this equation.

Nonetheless, Deuteronomy has on its side the character of the God that we find described in both testaments. This God is not inert or removed from what happens to human beings in space and time. The Bible portrays God as involved, concerned, and caring about people's joys and pains. The lesson that Israel read out of its peak experiences, above all the experience of the Exodus and establishment in its own land, was that its God was liberating and saving. By implication, therefore, Israel could expect good things from a right relationship to this God.

We may think that expressing such a conviction in terms such as prospering on the land and seeing the defeat of one's enemies is too crude to fit either the freedom of God or the tangledness of history. We should probably cringe when we hear football coaches praying for victory and see baseball players crossing themselves in the batter's box. Even when such prayers are more for the well-being of the players than for victory, they seem to vulgarize faith by bringing it down into pettiness and sweat. Similarly, we probably should cringe when we find people expecting that faith will bring them gains in the stock market and a shiny new car. But on some level the biblical God surely does promise reward for genuine faith, and certainly Jesus encourages people to ask God for bread (like children who know they will not get a stone: Matt. 7:9). The matter of benefits from faith therefore is quite tricky. The life and death of which Deuteronomy speaks admit of many different levels of interpretation.

The level at which I feel most comfortable is very basic. It seems to me that the overall portrait of the biblical God would be vitiated if there were no ultimate justice. If it made no final difference whether one was honest or dishonest, loving or hateful, the biblical God would mean nothing to our human enterprise, since all would be moral chaos. In my view the Bible, therefore, guarantees that taking the divine instruction, the Torah, to heart will make humanity prosper in what is most crucial to it. Clinging to the divine mystery in trust that it will show itself parental, striving to do what is right even when it seems bootless, working for peace even when financial profits and personal promotions lie in other directions—these basic choices to try to be obedient will bring us life rather than death. When we look to the heroes who have remained steadfast, obeying both conscience and what they take to be the commandments of God, we find they exhibit a confidence that the life of the Spirit which they preserve and nourish by such obedience is more important than the material diminishments, including even physical death, that their obedience can bring.

One thinks of Socrates, whom Plato cast as the figure who might have saved Athens had the city known what the spirit, conscience, genuine cultural prosperity, wisdom, and all the rest that life summarizes were all about. One thinks of Jesus, who went beyond even fidelity to conscience and died with compassion in his heart and forgiveness on his lips. In our day an Alexsandr Solzhenitsyn is so much more alive than the brutal regime that truth forced him to oppose that even though that regime cast him out of his beloved native land the world rightly counts him the victor. In our day the prisons of South Africa house many people who know a source of life that seems dead among their oppressors.

At this deep, if not ultimate, level of confrontation, people have to decide whether the light still shines in the darkness or the darkness has overcome it. Deuteronomy is a ringing declaration that obedience to God and the way of life is worth all the pain. It is a ringing declaration that the people will not be Israel, will not show the world what actually gives creation and history their meaning, unless the people keep faith with their sole God and the divine words of loving instruction.

Perhaps this last point is the one that those working for peace and justice should most emphasize. Even when we are not *in extremis*, when we are not driven to prison by our convictions and facing martyrdom, we can experience that God's way is a genuine, properly demanding way of growth in understanding and love. Stripped of the barbarities that the underdevelopment of some of the biblical authors tossed into it, the portrait of the biblical God stresses life and growth. Indeed, it stresses loving commitment to humanity on the model of a nursing mother or an inmost breath that takes over our prayer and compensates for all our weakness. We must read Deuteronomy in concert with Exodus and recall that the God making all of the demands of the Torah is the God who promised to be with the people and to reveal the divine nature in their time.

Consider the lilies of the field, their mode of growth. Consider the kingdom of God, how Jesus describes it. In more places than we may realize, people keep going on, keep telling the truth, keep trying to make things better. The kindest way to view many of our politicians and bureaucrats is to think that they keep a better future possible by caring for basic survival today. The same with most parents, teachers, and healers: They give God more time in which to make it clear that obedience to Torah is salvific. The only gross enemies of God are those who reject Deuteronomy's call to choose life.

What place does the land have in the Deuteronomic concept of life?

What is a proper conception of the rewards and punishments entailed in the two ways, the way of life and the way of death?

How does imagining God to be a nursing mother or an inmost breath soften the Deuteronomic legalism?

II

Prophets

The Word of God for the Cure of Evil Times

11

Divine Rule

1 Samuel 2:1–10

We now enter into the second section of the Hebrew Bible, which deals with materials that had gained scriptural status by about 200 B.C.E. This first text, as we implied when we indicated the sweep of the Deuteronomistic history, bears an affinity to the Book of Deuteronomy, even though we now locate it among the Former Prophets. The text is somewhat familiar from Luke 1:46–55, Mary's Magnificat, which was based largely upon the song of Hannah. Luke was drawing a parallel between the joy raised by a longed-for birth in the Old Testament and the joy raised by the pending birth of Jesus. We must criticize the text for its facile division of people into friends of God and enemies, as well as for the vengeance that it attributes to God, both of which are Deuteronomic staples. At the same time, the text is quite moving in the way that it makes the poor the apple of God's eye, as well as quite provocative in the way that it suggests that God's justice can contradict worldly measures of failure and success.

We may note first that Hannah, who felt herself humiliated if not indeed cursed by God because of her barrenness, had prayed long and hard for this birth. Her exultation therefore has good credentials, for she is no "Johanna-come-lately." One might translate the Deuteronomic theology into a spirituality that Hannah could champion, saying that those who trust in God, who turn their lives over to God, will gain an exultation, a spiritual joy, that will reward all their prayer and fasting. Among the Christian spiritual masters, joy and peace have been taken as the key signs of the Spirit of God, so much so that they could guide at least the first portions of any process of discernment. The further implication, quite important for any theological estimate of what human beings have been made for, is that union with God and experience of God are the basis of our deepest satisfactions.

Hannah is convinced that God is unique, in both holiness and reliability. God is her rock and her salvation; whom should she fear? And it is instructive that this testimony immediately leads Hannah to caution against pride and arrogance. Those who take their joy from God, who center their lives on God, are very sensitive to the presumption, the disorder, the real, if not always intended, arrogance of people who live as though God were not the sole Creator and Lord. Such people propose and think that they dispose, but the believer finds everything to depend upon God. Such people think that, since they have planted and watered, they give the increase; but the believer finds all increase, all successful outcome, to depend upon God. So the believer, like Hannah, thinks of human beings as servants who, even when they have performed well, have only done what God should have been able to expect of them. As verse 3 concludes, God is the one who has the knowledge of how history really is unfolding, and God is the one who weighs what actions are truly meritorious.

It is for this reason that the bows of those who think themselves mighty archers are broken; whether their arrows hit the mark of true significance is for God to judge. Similarly, it is for this reason that the people we may think feeble can have great strength. We do well to remember the primacy of God's judgments and the secondary character of our own judgments when it comes to evaluating how downtrodden or poor the victims of war and injustice are. By God's standards, they may stand much higher than their oppressors. Since God does not equate right with worldly might, these victims may be saints, with all the rights and honors accrued to sainthood, while their oppressors may be sinners, with all the debilities and liens attached thereto. This sort of rectification of worldly judgments is not, of course, any reason to slacken off from the labor of reducing the number of victims of injustice and the depth of the sufferings that warfare brings. But it is a reason to take a deeper breath and let one's lungs fill with hope: What one sees on the battlefield or on the federal assistance rolls is not the final word.

Verse 5 makes this line of thought bear on food and children, two of the primary specifications of the Bible's great passion for life. Just as God gave manna in the wilderness, the God to whom Hannah prays somehow, in some way, will feed the hungry and punish those who prosper unjustly. Similarly, the woman who thought her fertility something for which she could take credit will learn of a barrenness more befitting her pride, while the humble woman who bemoaned her barrenness and turned her face to the true Giver of life will bring forth abundantly.

The Song of Hannah is another fine illustration of the utopian imagination we described when meditating on the Jubilee year decreed in Leviticus 25. What Hannah describes has to be in the no-place of God's justice, the otherworldly realm of God's reign. With God, light and darkness no longer will be intermingled. In heaven, there will be reward for the good and punishment for the wicked.

Verses 6 and 7 express the same conviction in different images. God is the one who gives life or takes it away. God is the source of riches and the ultimate sanctioner of poverty. For people who believe in God, all human judgments on success and failure, on riches and poverty, are at best penultimate. Human use of such terms, all human concern with such evaluations, should be in fact become symbolic; that is, should become a way of turning what happens toward the mystery of God, which remains impenetrable and sovereign even when we have such guides to its general character as the Torah and the gospel. Neither the Torah nor the gospel takes away the sovereignty of God. Neither allows people to know with certitude how they stand with God; that is, whether they are saved. Both do, of course, present God as eager to save, longing to give the Spirit to hearts open in welcome. But all of the saints, from Hannah to Paul, place justification in God, not in themselves. All in fact feel better not having to be responsible for their own salvation, because they think God a much better guarantor.

Hannah does, however, think that God has a special love and concern for the poor. If only because the poor are so many and have no other real recourse but God, God must think of them with delight and love to raise them from their wretchedness. How we reconcile this divine desire with the manifest tendency of biological evolution and human history alike to produce wholesale suffering is a very great intellectual problem. But on the level of faith, which finally must undercut intellectual wrestlings and demand a summary yes or no to a life that none of us will ever fully comprehend, the posture of exemplars such as Hannah is very instructive. After many dark nights, Hannah is sure that God cares for poor or ordinary people like herself. She is more than willing to leave reward and punishment in God's hands.

Just as God is patient with the temptations to despair and the cries of anger that injustice and suffering raise everywhere, so should we be patient. But we may console ourselves in our own personal experiences of injustice and our own doubts about whether work for peace does any real good at all that the saints drew from their encounters with God (encounters often much more harrowing than ours) the strength to write God a blank check.

The carte blanche discernible in so many holy lives is a letting go of all false responsibilities for history, all temptations to play God. It takes considerable wisdom, of course, to know the difference between the things we must leave to God and the things that are our own proper responsibility. But a self-reliant time always needs the corrective of true religion, which at least glimpses how things stand under the aspect of eternity, just as an irresponsible time always needs the corrective of Genesis 1:28, where divine instruction makes it plain that what happens to the earth very much lies on our heads. The ironic and ultimately consoling fact, of course, is that every time is both too self-reliant and irresponsible. Everyone of us has to learn when to push and when to let go.

How does the prayer of Hannah make God the champion of the poor?

At what point should believers leave reward and punishment in God's hands?

What does the example of Hannah say about petitionary prayer?

12

Personal Sin

2 Samuel 11:26–12:7

Chapters 9–20 of Second Samuel are by consensus the high point of literary narrative in the Old Testament. Because of their portrait of David, he has come down to us as the most vivid character in the Old Testament. The more carefully literary analysts study this section, the more they come away convinced that the author was a brilliant psychologist and artist. The covenant that Israel associated with David drew much of its strength from this memoir, because if God could be thought to have pledged an unconditional, never-failing support of the Davidic line even though from the beginning that line was flawed by sin, then divine grace truly was free, and the limitations of the Deuteronomic theology (where, as we have seen, grace is tied to obedience and good works) were overcome.

The first impression we get from the story of David and Bathsheba is that the king has verified Lord Acton's judgment that power corrupts. No longer the simple shepherd described in 1 Samuel, David now is able to satisfy any desire that comes upon him. He desires Bathsheba, and this desire takes him to the extreme of committing adultery with her and arranging the murder of Uriah the Hittite, her husband. As the parable of Nathan suggests, David had a bevy of wives in the royal harem, while Uriah had only Bathsheba. The problem with power like that of a king is that it allows the untowardness of one's desires to break out and easily gain their end. Few people will stand up to the powerful, so the powerful can develop moral amnesia and forget the basic rules of self-restraint.

The parable, which seems somewhat contrived, allows David to grasp the dynamics of his own situation in an external form. He does not immediately realize the application to himself, but when Nathan drives the connection home David has been prepared to accept it. Ancient cultures such as the Greek used the theater as an external forum in which the people might see the great issues facing them as citizens and private individuals alike. Greek tragedy was like a communal examination of conscience and psychotherapy. Good teaching and preaching in every era have been similarly astute in using examples, case studies, and stories. One thinks, for instance, of the parables of Jesus. For two thousand years, Westerners have thought about neighborliness in the images of the parable of the Good Samaritan. In the same way, they have thought about ingratitude, repentance, and the unconditional love of God in the images of the parable of the prodigal son. Perhaps this means that our work for peace and justice will only be as effective as the stories we can fashion to dramatize it.

For all of his power and status, King David had to put up with the counter-institution of prophecy. There is no indication here that he was unwilling to do this, but the history of Israelite kingship that we find in First and Second Kings shows that many times ruler and prophet were at loggerheads. One thinks, for instance, of the mortal danger that the prophet Elijah risked by opposing Ahab and Jezebel. One thinks, as well, of John the Baptist, who lost his head because he rebuked King Herod. Despite these times when the biblical prophets risked death, their tradition gave them a solid right to work. Biblical religion evidently felt it a good thing, a sign of health, for there to be checks and balances, or even a loyal opposition, encoded in the covenantal scheme of things. This does not mean that Nathan did not have to be courageous. David could very well have lashed out at one who showed him his sin and called him to repentance. But it does mean that David felt pressures to listen to one who fitted the typology of the traditional mouthpiece of God. David in fact became the ideal king in later Israelite interpretation precisely because he did so honor the word of God, did repent and return to his earlier conviction that everything he or Israel had was a gift of the divine bounty.

Those who work for peace and justice inevitably come into conflict with the forces in whose interest it is to continue preparing for war and to maintain the prevailing patterns of injustice. The past twenty-five years in the United States have been an object lesson in how such a conflict is likely to go. When the industrial-military complex, as President Eisenhower presciently described it, is the predominant combine in the land, those who are moved by the plight of the poor to call for a reform of the going economic system and those who are moved by the specter of nuclear war to call for a reform of the going policy of deterrence (m.a.d.: mutual assured destruction) are almost sure to find themselves attacked as unpatriotic, Marxist, or utopian. In fact, they may simply be people who have read their Bible, listened to Jesus and the other prophets, pondered the statements of the national council of their church, and concluded that peace and justice are God's will. For their comfort, they may recall that the prophets, too, were mocked and discredited by the powerholders they threatened and that Jesus himself was hated by the establishment. This does not immediately legitimate every word and work of peacemakers, but it does give them a good lineage in which to place themselves.

What Nathan does for David is make him realize that he is the man to whom the story applies. Because David is more than an adulterer, more than a ruler obsessed with his own image and power, David can hear Nathan's teaching, can feel Nathan's rebuke, and act upon it. This is clear from his response later in 12:13: "I have sinned against the Lord." In his charge, Nathan had accused David of despising the word of the Lord and doing evil in God's sight. Both Nathan's charge and David's acceptance of it bear further meditation.

When we or powerholders whom we accuse do evil—abet injustice and ease the way to war—we despise the word of God. Often we have fallen to such a sorry state of conscience, to such a moral deafness, that we scarcely realize we are doing this. We slide into the assumption that what we do in the workaday world is our business and that the word of God is something which pertains only to Sundays. Many of the people who play the dramatic parts in the global tragedy of economic injustice and warmongering show up in churches or houses of prayer on the appointed holy days. The rest of the week, however, they consider themselves realists, pragmatists, who deal with things the way they truly are and eschew the luxury of thinking that public affairs might have a place for mercy, forgiveness, or dealing with enemies as though they were not all wicked and as if we could make a new beginning with them.

The cynicism we find in the worst of the warmongers and tyrants does in fact strike the believer as a great despising of God's word. From Hitler and Stalin to the leaders of present-day regimes that torture dissidents, murder priests and ministers who preach the gospel, and try to justify racism or an economy that siphons off 75 percent of the nation's wealth for the benefit of less than 25 percent of the nation's population, the last half-century has shown us a despising of God, at times an outright hatred of God, that truly is chilling. As in the time of Cain, the earth cries out at the blood spilled upon it, and if the earth were to swallow up the great evildoers we could only count it justice.

True, it is not for us to take God's place as judge and start naming saints and sinners, but it is for us—for any people of conscience—to read the signs of the times and discern what fruits different positions are growing. I take it as a small exercise in discernment to study the competing arguments of the columnists who populate the editorial pages of my newspaper to try to determine which ones square with the prophetic theology of the Bible. Almost always I find that neither liberals nor conservatives do an adequate job. Almost always the prophetic theology of the Bible implies the more radical possibility that we are the people who have sinned against the Lord.

How could David—the adulterer, the murderer—become Israel's model king?

How does Nathan turn David around?

How close is the link between militarism or dictatorship and despising the word of God?

13

Prophecy

1 Kings 19:1–13

We have seen the effect of the prophet Nathan on the good king David. In the present text we see the effect of the bad rulers Ahab and Jezebel on the prophet Elijah. Once again the literary context is the Deuteronomistic history, which is structured by a pattern of Israelite apostasy from the obligations of the covenant and God's consequent punishment. A submotif, however, is the clash between the prophets who maintain the truth of God's word and the kings who try to ignore it.

Elijah is the most famous of the nonwriting prophets; and, as we see in this text, he is "jealous for the Lord, the God of hosts." This phrase, which is repeated in verse 14 at a second encounter with God, serves as a sort of password. Since Elijah can say it in full honesty, it protects him in his encounters with God. In the background is the notion that the true divinity itself is jealous concerning Israel. God has made a covenant that binds the people to place their trust only in him. Elijah is implying that he has served this desire of the true God and has tried to make Israel honor the contract the people have made to live by.

A second overtone in this phrase is a contrast between the faith of Elijah and the faith of Jezebel. The queen has opposed the God of the covenant, thinking that a greater prosperity would come to her realm from worshiping Baal, the god of her native Phoenicia. Baal was allied with another fertility divinity, Asherah (see 1 Kings 18:19), so the faith of

Jezebel was polytheistic. The "God of hosts" whom Elijah worships is the sole God, the sovereign over all of the forces that Baal, Asherah, and other fertility deities represent. The clash therefore is between theologies as well as cultural traditions. Elijah is standing up for the worldview passed down to him from Abraham and Moses, according to which only one God rules nature and history. The implication is that, because only one God rules nature and history, both realms are not chaotic but orderly; they are zones of divine providence.

In contrast, the worldview of Jezebel makes what happens in nature and history the casual, accidental result of the clashes and alliances among the very many physical and spiritual forces that the various gods represent. Elijah is persecuted not only because he wants to keep Israel true to its identity, as its most hallowed traditions define this identity. He is also persecuted because he champions a sole God whose admission would require sinners such as Ahab and Jezebel to bring their untoward allegiances and their murderous conduct into line.

We can say, then, that Elijah shows what can happen when one confronts powerful people who are not about to bow their heads to a Creator and Savior who makes strong demands on their consciences. His life in peril, Elijah has to flee into the wilderness. I recall meeting Stanley Rother, the first American missionary slain in Central America, when he was in flight from the (American-supported) government in Guatemala. He had learned that his name was on a list of those soon to be executed, so he left the poor Indians among whom he had labored for many years and returned to Oklahoma. Some months later he thought that it was safe for him to return. Guatemala had become his home, and the Indians had become his Christian community. But Rother underestimated the threat that the government saw in his work with the Indians, the fear the government had that this work would spotlight their many injustices to such native peoples whom they had cast to the margins, so he lost his life to a death squad that came in the night. The government tried to frame Rother's community and make them seem his murderers, but his community grieved for him as for their father and soon they began revering his bodily remains as those of a martyr and saint.

In his wilderness, Elijah feels heavy depression and thinks himself as good as dead. He wants to lay down the burden of the unfair fight he has had to suffer; he wants to curl up and join his ancestors in the ground. We recall the bone-weariness that some of the writing prophets evidence. Prophets are not necessarily people who love the limelight or find their energy in conflict. Sometimes they hate the clashes into which they are drawn and feel that their conscience is a tyrant. Nonetheless, they carry on, speaking the judgments and making the protests that their consciences require.

The angel of the Lord who comes to succor Elijah and restore his strength symbolizes the help that the prophets and saints regularly receive. It comes to them unexpectedly, as though, having staggered to the abyss of hopelessness, they tipped over and fell in only to find that the darkness housed a strange updraft. The Spirit of God is like a buoyancy that keeps us from going under.

When the psychologist Erik Erikson studied the life of Mahatma Gandhi, who led India to freedom from British rule, Erikson found that Gandhi seemed to have looked the nothingness of his own strength and the apparent feebleness of his people's power right in the face and drawn strength from the fact that he could rely only on the power of Truth.

The people who flee crises that they should face never give God a chance to provide them this experience. The people who face their problems, their sins, and the stone walls that seem to be blocking their way and try to compose their souls in a bedrock realism often feel peace and strength wash their fears away. It would be mere whistling in the dark to speak of this possibility, let alone to suggest that one can rely on its occurring, were there not such a strong testimony to it by the saints. Indeed, Luke 12:11–12 makes the support of the Spirit a promise of Jesus himself: "When they bring you before the synagogues and the rulers and the authorities, do not be anxious how or what you are to answer or what you are to say; for the Holy Spirit will teach you in that very hour what you ought to say."

Strengthened by the angel (the spiritual power) of God,

Elijah is able to trek forty days and nights to a faraway place associated with the holy revelations of God (for the Deuteronomistic tradition, Horeb was where God communicated with Moses). The theophany— manifestation of God— that then occurs is both a consolation for Elijah and an instruction in the nature of the true God. Elijah feels that his life is threatened, and justifiably so: Jezebel has slain most of his fellow prophets. God consoles him for the burdens he has borne on behalf of God's cause. No matter how great the power of Jezebel to inflict death, the very Source of all life will stand by him and render Jezebel's power weak.

The instruction that follows elaborates just how the Source of life, the Creator of the world, prefers to communicate the divine presence. Elijah stands on the mountain, much as Moses had, and the attentive reader recalls the fearsome majesty of the theophany associated with making the covenant (see Ex. 19). But here the divine comfort does not come in the wind or the earthquake or the fire. God's chosen way here is a still, small voice that comes after all the banging and clatter. Just as for Moses and the people of his time the most significant presence of God was in the words of the covenant (above all, the Ten Commandments) that were the heart of the theophany on Sinai, so here Elijah realizes that the holiest time is when the still, small voice touches his spirit. He wraps his face in his mantle (tradition said that no one could see God and live) and comes out to attend to whatever God wants to say to him. God asks him what he is doing there, and Elijah repeats his plight. Then God gives him his further commission, promising that his future work will prosper. The prophet has revealed his weakness and been upheld.

This passage should be a classic for those who want to derive their work for peace and justice from a life of honest prayer. Elijah, the prototypical accuser of wicked authority, is willing to pray to God when he feels in mortal distress, and he is able to bear God's response. Elijah can say that his great concern really has been God's cause. When asked why we are where we are, we too need only be able to say, "For God's sake."

How should ordinary believers be jealous for the Lord, the God of Hosts?

What does Elijah suggest about the relations between prophecy and secular power?

When did you last hear the still, small voice of God?

14

Messianic Peace

Isaiah 9:2–7

Although Amos is usually considered the first of the prophets whose oracles and teachings were written down, Isaiah of Jerusalem is the oldest of the authors whose materials now appear among the Latter Prophets whom Jewish tradition has considered major—Isaiah, Jeremiah, and Ezekiel. It seems that Isaiah of Jerusalem was active during the period from 740 to 701 B.C.E., a time when the major concerns were the Syro-Ephraimite war of 734–732 and the threats that Assyria posed to Jerusalem in the years 734–701 (in 721 Assyria conquered the Northern Kingdom). Our text occurs in the first part (chapters 1–39) of a book that present-day scholarship usually divides into three parts (chapters 1–39, 40–55, and 56–66). Consequently, it is attributed to First Isaiah. Within First Isaiah, chapters 1–12 often are considered prophecies against Judah and Jerusalem. The prophet is warning his people about what the threats of foreign invasion portend, and he is calling for a return to true religion. Although our text may in fact have been stimulated by the prophet's experience of the good, reforming King Hezekiah (ruled 727–698), in it the prophet's imagination stretches out to picture what a full reign by God's anointed ruler (''Messiah'') would be like.

Generations of Bible-readers have been moved by the poetry of Isaiah, not the least of whose famous passages is this one from chapter 9. Even today many readers are bound to hear it in the cadences of Handel's *Messiah,* as it has been played year after year before Christmas. The power of any biblical poetry comes from its movement between the actual, truly historical circumstances in which it first arose and the myriad later circumstances to which it applies.

Just as the Deuteronomistic historians dealt with such events of the past as the Exodus as paradigms, experiences that should be considered privileged indications of God's intentions at all times and places, so the prophets created language that might illumine any time and place with the light of God's proven character. Thus in Isaiah 9:2 one might legitimately think of darkness as either the foreboding that the prospect of foreign invasion had raised or the foreboding that just about any historical period gives grounds for fearing. One might, for instance, think today of the threat of nuclear warfare that darkens all horizons. The light that comforts people walking in darkness can bear similarly diverse overtones. It can be the light of Hezekiah, whose virtue and wisdom were bulwarks at the time of Assyrian menace. It can be the light of God's fidelity, which seemed to suggest that God might send an ideal ruler who would free Israel from all threat. And today it can be the Johannine light shining in the darkness and always proving stronger.

Dwelling in the light of his hope, the prophet sees Israel blessed and rejuvenated. The multiplication of the nation recalls the command of Genesis to increase and be fruitful. The people will feel that God has been gracious to them, as they feel at the time of harvest when the earth has smiled and winter bears no threats, or as they feel after a victory in battle. The military imagery continues in verse 4, again tying the prophecy to the specific threats of invasion by Assyria. The reference to Midian recalls the victory of Gideon commemorated in Judges 7:15–25. Yet verse 5 moves beyond victory in war to envision a state of peace, a state in which the boots and tunics of soldiers will be fuel for the fire. Although Isaiah is indebted to the Israelite tradition of holy warfare and so thinks victory in battle a gift of God tokening the divine favor, he moves beyond this tradition and obviously thinks that a better gift of God would be a state in which warfare were unnecessary, passé, burned out.

In their conflicts with people who support preparations for war, sometimes by invoking the necessity of defending freedoms given by God and required for proper religion, peacemakers rooted in the Bible can use Isaiah as a good example of the unequal levels at which the two visions, victory in battle and no need for battle, stand in the prophets. Isaiah may tolerate battle for the sake of saving the chosen people and defeating gross injustice, but his greater love and hope is peace, which he considers more worthy of God.

The leader who might bring such a peace obviously is a figure of utopian imagination. Late in the Precommon Era Israel did long for an actual deliverer, and throughout the history of Judaism in the Common Era there were spasms of messianic expectation. But the main thrust and value of this passage is that which we have already associated with the utopian imagination. It carries the conviction of faith that, when things are as they must be in God's sight, peace and justice will flow abundantly. The child whom the prophet imagines is more the scion of this conviction than the heir of the Davidic kingly line. The government to be upon his shoulder is more the reign of God, as the New Testament will call it, than the execution of any earthly rule.

For biblical theology, the name of God or any other significant spiritual reality brings human beings into contact with that reality. Israel never has God's name delivered to it (see Ex. 3:14), because that would encourage attempts to manipulate the divine name as though human beings might control God. But the prophets and the other biblical poets feel free to produce namings that might catch something of the divine reality without destroying the divine mystery. So the names given here—Wonderful Counselor, Mighty God, and the rest—are intended as metaphors that might stir up worship and hope. They do not give any reader a sure fix on either God or the divine intentions for history, but the canonization of the scripture in which they appear means that Judaism and Christianity have considered them accredited as trustworthy clues.

The first name, Wonderful Counselor, befits the interests of the wisdom schools and writers who were influential after the return from exile. No doubt they had forebears in the time of Isaiah of Jerusalem, since wisdom certainly was a long-standing interest of Egypt and other of Israel's ancient neighbors. But the image of guidance and of knowledge of how things move in nature and so should move in Israel fully comes into influence in the postexilic period. So this name probably pleased the canonical editors of Isaiah, who were working around 200 B.C.E., suggesting to them that those who would best token the advent of God's reign would carry the practical good sense of people who had mounted up toward heaven, where the most important counsel reposed.

The other names suggest the exalted status of both the leaders who would bring the reign of God near and the reign itself. "Mighty God" understandably has been taken literally in Christian circles, but it can also connote "divine, godlike in might." "Everlasting Father" combines the warmth of familial affection with the stability and the durability of more-than-earthly status. And "Prince of Peace" definitely associates the ideal ruler with order and tranquillity, improving on the old cluster of images that saw the leader of the people as its foremost warrior (which could mean its most efficient butcher).

The final verse expands on this ideal peace and ties it to the golden throne of David. Both the peace of God and the rule of David have to be endless, uncorrupted by mortality, if the utopian imagination is to be satisfied. Note the explicit inclusion of justice and the concluding attribution of everything to the Lord of hosts, who is zealous for Israel's full prospering and must be believed to be seeking actively a full justice and peace.

The main lesson I would read out of Isaiah 9 today is its reminder that the reign of God, the time when divine justice and peace fully prevail, is surpassingly beautiful. It implies a government whose simple contemplation would improve the very imperfect governments we now experience. It suggests that intimacy with the God of covenantal promises can stabilize the hopes of all who are longing for justice and peace, telling them that the beauty they want to save is not illusory.

In what sense is the Messiah a figure of utopian imagination?
How should poetry nourish religious hope?
Why is peace a central feature of the reign of God?

15

Punishment

Isaiah 13:9–16

Chapters 13–23 of the Book of Isaiah contain oracles preached against the foreign nations that threatened Israel. Here the references to Babylon and the Medes (Isa. 13:1, 17) suggest a time around 562 B.C.E., when Assyria had yielded power to Babylon and Judah was in exile. If so, we would be dealing with materials preached in the spirit of Isaiah of Jerusalem rather than by that prophet himself. Our text shows that a passion for punishing wrongdoers, or even for obtaining vengeance against one's enemies, was not limited to the Torah. In the prophets the same emotions frequently appear, and those who would use the Bible as their first instruction in what God is like have to struggle with the problem of reconciling divine vengeance with divine justice and mercy.

The "day of the Lord" mentioned in verse 9 is a term also used by Amos (8:9–10), Jeremiah (30:5–7), and other prophets (see Obad. 15; Joel 1:15; Zeph. 1:14–18; Mal. 4:5–6). Generally, the use of this term before the exile to Babylon makes it a warning to Israel: repent, because God will soon judge your sins and render strong punishment. During and after the Exile it tends to refer to the foreign nations that have oppressed Israel, assuring both them (should they be listening) and Israel that the one God everywhere will visit wrath upon evildoers. Here, then, the probability is that the oracle seeks to assure both Israel and Babylon that Judgment Day is coming. That would be a comfort of sorts to Israelites suffering depression and affliction, and it would be a grim warning to any Babylonians with ears to hear. Babylon was, in fact, defeated by Persia in 529, and shortly thereafter the Israelites were free to return to Judah.

The passage describes Judgment Day as something afflicting the whole earth. Nature enters into God's wrathful coming, reminding us that the people of the biblical period had considerably closer ties with nature than modern urbanites usually do. The Bible thinks of God as the first, quite direct, cause of what happens in nature. It has none of the mentality developed by modern science, according to which God is at most a force that started things in the beginning and secondary, finite causes are the real matter of interest. The Koran, like the Bible, depicts Judgment Day in cosmological terms. When the one God of nature and history arrives on the day of reckoning, the heavens and the earth, the stars and the seas, all will tremble in fear. A darkness like that which preceded God's creation of light (God is the sole source of light, both that in nature and that in human conscience) will foretell the punishment that the wicked will receive on Judgment Day. It will be a darkness all the worse for human beings who have had the light and have not used it well.

Notice the string of attributes which the prophet lays out in verse 11. The wicked of the earth will be punished for their evil, their iniquity, their pride, their arrogance, their haughtiness, their ruthlessness. The last four attributes seem to coalesce and relate to the first three as cause to effect. Wickedness, evil, and iniquity (three names for the same basic disorder and wrongdoing), all stem from the creature's not keeping to its place in the divine scheme of things. Disorder comes when people do not realize their nothingness, their total dependence on God, and so act as though they themselves were the lords of the earth. The humility that the Bible considers so important, the "fear of the Lord" which is the beginning of wisdom, is nothing craven or ignoble. It is the state of awareness that any appreciation of the bedrock truth ought to generate. The bedrock truth of the human condition is that we are mortal, finite, ignorant, and often twisted. The bedrock truth is that if we are the final power in the world the world is in horrible shape. We come from the darkness of prebirth, which we do not understand, and we go into the darkness of death, which we also do not understand. Had we the slightest bit of sense, we would consider our time in the light a wondrous mystery and do our best to show the One who gave it to us that the gift was not a terrible mistake.

This biblical analysis of the human condition remains completely valid today, despite the fact that one seldom hears it or anything like its equivalent in our schools or even in many of our churches. We are no less mortal than our forebears and no less in the dark about the mysteries of life and death. The biological and medical advances that we have made are wonderful, and I mean no discredit to the people of great mind and heart who have benefitted millions through them. But these advances remain at a level well above the bedrock issues encoded in the human spirit. At the end of the twentieth century C.E., as at the beginning of the twentieth century B.C.E., the first order of business for humanity is to appropriate its mortality and ignorance and thereby gain a proper humility.

The physical descriptions of the day of the Lord that occur in the middle verses of our text spell out the prophet's sense of what the visitation of justice upon the wicked would be like. The limits of his theology at this point, like the limits of the theology of any other period at most points, are the limits of the imagination it can muster. Today we must think of the universe as immeasurably more vast than what a prophet gazing at the heavens more than twenty-five hundred years ago could even suspect. We know of galaxies upon galaxies, to the sum of millions of light-years away. We do not know, or have a solid scientific consensus about, how the universe will end, just as we cannot answer the related question of how the universe began. Even if there was a big bang of hydrogen at the outset and the character of the universe was set in the first milliseconds, it remains a mystery why the bang should have occurred and what the final stage of the process that it initiated will look like.

In my view, the only thing that biblical theology can say about the relation between Judgment Day and present-day cosmology is that the God who alone makes some sense of the whole must be eminently moral as well as powerful. In other words, justice is as much a requirement as order or explanation on a physical level. The problem of evil and how we are to gain a balanced reconciliation to it is as much a part of the cosmic puzzle as is the problem of how the universe began, now runs, and will end.

Faith that God will deal with the problem of evil, like faith that God does have a meaningful end in store for the universe, reposes on the character of the God in whom one believes. This makes the final verses of our text all the more problematic, of course, since a God who would dash infants to pieces before their parents' eyes does not give us much confidence that the universe is in good hands. I prefer, therefore, to be quite frank about the human character of much of the biblical literature and say that here is a place where we have to criticize the human authors and make sure that their defects are not transferred onto God.

So, too, in our work for peace and justice. While we can take comfort in believing that evildoers will be punished and innocent sufferers will be recompensed, we have to remember that Israel's better God was slow to anger and quick to forgive all people and that Christ on the cross died for all in a consummate expression of the outreach of the divine mercy and love. Our God cannot be a destroyer of any people's children, a ravisher of any people's women. Unless our God is on the side of all people's protection against such evils, we aren't likely to continue believing. Unless our God verifies Plato's equation of divinity with goodness, we are not likely to make our work for peace and justice a religious service. Ultimately, the proper punishment of evildoers seems to come in their inevitable alienation from God. By choosing evil and rejecting God's Spirit of honesty and love, they enter a hell of absurdity and self-destruction. The call of God that makes them human no longer sounds, and they put themselves in a moral universe as cold as the cosmic dust.

What place does punishment have in the reign of God?

What are the positive benefits that can result from confessing our mortality and ignorance?

Why does the denial of God make the universe a moral void?

16

Victimhood

Isaiah 53:1–6

Chapters 40–55, associated with Second Isaiah, make most sense if one locates them during the exile in Babylon—that is, before the conquest of Babylon by Persia that allowed the Jews to return home in 538 B.C.E. Our text in chapter 53 is one of the famous songs about the servant of God through whose contemplation Second Isaiah can think through the meaning of Israel's victimhood. The prophet probably has in mind collective Israel, insofar as the people have stayed faithful to God and so have suffered in the hope of redeeming the Exile from meaninglessness. It was nearly inevitable, however, that Christians would interpret the servant as an anticipation of the suffering Christ—as a type that Jesus fulfilled.

For our purposes, the main point is the new ground that Second Isaiah breaks. In his servant we glimpse the possibility that God's way of healing the world back to peace and justice is by transforming innocent suffering, the apparently worst result of creation and history, into something so pure that it becomes a central revelation of the divine love.

Chapter 53 begins by putting the reader on notice that its message will seem astounding. The prophet has heard intimations of a special meaning in the Exile, but he doubts that many of his contemporaries will recognize what he is reporting. The "arm" of the Lord is the power of God, the strength through which divinity chooses to work its will. Has God ever before made it known that the divine mode of operation could be through weakness, even through defeat?

The one who grew up before God like a young plant could be the Israel now suffering in exile, or it could be any victim whose suffering God chooses to use. We have previously noted that the Bible is scripture in good part because its metaphors are always relevant and suggestive. The figure of a root out of dry ground suggests an entity of little account, although if we stress the word *root* the implication may be that from this dusty thing magnificent blossoms will flower. The main burden of verse 2, however, is to convey the unprepossessingness of the victim who will prove to be a source of grace and healing. The victim was not the sort who would draw admiring glances. On the contrary, the suggestion is that the victim was ugly and ignored by others.

In Grace Mojtabai's fine novel *The Four Hundred Eels of Sigmund Freud* (New York: Simon and Schuster, 1976), the main character grates on other people's nerves to the point that they reject him utterly and he finally commits suicide. It seems no accident that he is named Isaiah. The long lament, an apparently retrospective self-accusation, in verse 3 would fit this fictional Isaiah, as well as many of the people whom history has rejected if not martyred: "He was despised and rejected by men; a man of sorrows, and acquainted with grief; and as one from whom men hide their faces he was despised, and we esteemed him not."

The suicide of the novel's Isaiah is the only act which redeems the community that has ostracized him. Because they are all forced to rethink the godless ambition that previously had driven them and because a few of the members actually reject it, Isaiah has not died in vain. Indeed, we might argue that without Isaiah's physical death the spiritual deaths of the entire community would have been virtually assured. The least attractive member, therefore, became the most crucial means of grace. For the biblical Isaiah, the similar thought seems to be that when Israel was in its least attractive hour, begrimed by the dust of servitude in Babylon and fouled by ill-use, God still had a purpose for Israel. Nothing, not even the worst humiliations, lay outside God's ability to communicate the divine love and so work healing.

Verse 4 is one of the most provocative verses, leading reflective people to wonder about the connections among human beings and how it might be that one innocent victim could bear the griefs and sorrows of many others. Certainly, this question goes to the heart of traditional Christology, which pondered deeply how Jesus on the cross could have been the crux of God's way of saving the world. But the question occurs in other contexts, too, when people ask whether waste, disease, and death are mere ugliness or whether even they might serve redemption.

As I write I have a particular death in mind, a particular person wasted by cancer. Her last weeks had little beauty in them, and she had to accept the final destruction of even her hope to end her life feeling that something round and full had come to term. Due to the love of her family and the good offices of people from the hospice movement, she did experience peace, and the quality of her life was long maintained. But like most deaths hers was far from obviously necessary or useful. And she died in her seventies, making one wonder all the more about those who die young. Could it be that her last weeks served God's purposes for her family and friends? Could it be that the Spirit was indeed moving in their depths, where they did not even know how to express the prayers too deep for words? Whether such things in fact happened, I do not know, but certainly they could have happened. Certainly when my own father died, even more prematurely, I came away thinking that he had made his death a final gift to me, a wonderfully consoling "fear not."

Where would we be if all of us did not die? Our sense of solidarity is thin enough even when we have mortality as an absolutely common denominator. What would we be like if our discrepancies, our bases for boasting, our foreignness as people of different geographic areas, different ethnic traditions, and different religions were the last word about us?

Even more provocatively, where would we be if God had remained wholly on the side of deathlessness? For the classical Greeks, mortality was the great divide between human beings and gods. Human beings were thoroughly framed by the fact that they were going to die, so the gods, being deathless, had to be of another order (and could not know the pathos of the human condition). At the boldness of its theological center, through what is technically called "the communication of idioms," orthodox Christianity, however, made the fusion of divinity and humanity in Jesus Christ so intimate that it sanctioned people's saying, "God died on the cross." Certainly this line of thought can be abused, for too many people already think of Jesus Christ as a divine being masquerading in human garb. It has, therefore, been necessary to stress the complete humanity of Jesus, his full likeness to us in all things save sin. But Isaiah's thought, combined with Jesus on the cross, also summons the strictly orthodox insight into the divine nature that God, the impassible Father, has found a way to take suffering to the bosom of divinity and make the cause of those who suffer divinity's own cause. This is a truly staggering possibility and one that throws a whole new light on what working on behalf of the victims of war and injustice can signify.

At the end of our passage, Isaiah makes the servant the bearer of the results of the waywardness, the iniquity, of his whole community. At the depths of our reflection, we are bound to notice that a great deal of human suffering comes from wars and inequities that human beings themselves cause—that is, comes from human sin. The Servant whom Christians adore took the sins of the world to himself and thereby took the sins of the world away. The victims whom Christians want to succor are best seen as members of the Body of this Servant. The agony that the whole Christ suffers in every age is defined by Jesus' death and resurrection two thousand years ago, although, of course, each pain continues to be woefully unique. But to say there is nothing redeeming pain is to say that history is obviously the tale of an idiot. All pain,. suffering, and victimhood by sin has an alternate paradigm waiting in the sanctuary. God and suffering humanity now intersect.

In what cautious sense is Isaiah 53 an anticipation of Jesus?

How valid is it to assimilate all suffering people to the servant of the Lord and to Jesus?

In what sense does God suffer human evildoing and thereby redeem it?

17

Inner Renewal

Jeremiah 31:29–34

For traditional Judaism, the most revelatory event in history was the exodus from Egypt and the gaining of the promised land. Each year the community commemorated this event and the grace of God that it disclosed through the feast of Passover. The Christian passover is the feast of Easter. There Christians have commemorated the exodus from sin and death and the gaining of grace and life that the Father worked through the crucifixion and resurrection of Jesus. There Jesus once again fulfills a type established in the Hebrew Bible. And if the text from Second Isaiah that we have just contemplated suggests the type for Jesus' crucifixion (the Suffering Servant), this text from Jeremiah suggests the type for Jesus' sending the Spirit into believers' hearts.

The first verses of our text reflect a discussion that we also find echoed in Deuteronomy 24:16 and Ezekiel 18. In the period 650–550 B.C.E., when Judah was contemplating the fall of Israel (the Northern Kingdom) to Assyria and the threats to its own sovereignty that finally were realized by its own fall to Babylon, the question of personal responsibility was much debated. Ought one to think of what happened in one's own generation as the result of what one's ancestors had done, or was the wiser counsel to look to oneself and stress personal responsibility?

Jeremiah, Deuteronomy, and Ezekiel all urged the latter course. Despite the obvious truth that one generation is the legatee of the previous generation, inheriting the consequences of prior actions both good and bad, the religious elite of Judah rejected the alienation of personal responsibility that such a truth could create. Unlike Hindu and Buddhist teachers, the Israelite prophets would sanction no doctrine of *karma* that might make today the slave of yesterday. The sharpness of the word that came to the Old Testament prophets cut to the innermost conscience of the person who received it. The freedom and personalism of the biblical God meant that God could uniquely address any situation and call for dialogue. Today was not just another point on the endless circle of a history that repeated itself *kalpa* after *kalpa* (to use the Indian term for the great units in which the gods parceled out cosmic history). If one heard God's voice today, one was under a personal imperative not to harden one's heart and think that word old hat. The God of Moses and Elijah could be utterly novel, and from this divine novelty came the possibility that each person could have a special identity and a singular role to play.

So for Jeremiah the taste in our mouths comes from the diet each of us has been following. If our teeth are set on edge, we ought first to look to our own sins. Equally, however, we ought to look to our own hearts for the spiritual encouragements, the active divine supports, that might make our special responsibilities or trials bearable.

Jeremiah is bold enough to describe a time when God will redo the covenant to take into account the personalism, the individual responsibility, that the prophets had come to realize is essential for mature religion. Note in verse 32 that the covenant made at the time of the Exodus is Jeremiah's paradigm and that he feels sufficiently moved by the new word that God has given him to change this most hallowed of traditional models. Although God had taken Israel by the hand out of Egypt and slavery, the people had broken their covenant with God. Although God had treated Israel as his bride, Israel had not responded. (Ezekiel and Hosea would say that Israel had acted adulterously.) So Jeremiah realized that something more powerfully gracious and more intimate had to be fashioned.

Just as Second Isaiah realized that suffering and victimhood demanded a deeper penetration of the divine love, so Jeremiah realized that if God wants a humanity fit to be a spouse, God is the one who will have to accomplish it.

The deepest point of Jeremiah's vision occurs in verse 33. The new covenant will make the law of God, the Torah, an interior matter, something written on believers' hearts so that they know instinctively that they belong to God, that God is identified with them, and that God is always on their side. At a stroke, then, Jeremiah has undercut the extrinsic nature and the legalism that always dogged the Mosaic covenant and the Deuteronomic theology. He has realized that people will only do what they ought and live as they ought when good behavior, or morality, is the overflow of what they really want to do. Jeremiah has realized what Confucius, his near contemporary in ancient China, realized: The Way and the self have to merge so that one has no untoward desires and really only wants to walk on the way.

Verse 34 brings home the further consequences. When God becomes the basic instructor of the people and the covenant is properly interiorized, the outward teachings that society imposes and requires are quite secondary. At the most, they are reminders of the divine promptings, elicitations of the performance that people know from the heart is required of them. Clearly, there are further things to be said about this very radical position, but for the moment we can let its radicalism stand.

The God of Jeremiah concludes this marvelous promise of a new, interiorized covenant by adding a pledge to forgive sin. When God is present to the people that God has graced to this degree, sin—disorder and lovelessness—will be a thing of the past. As we might translate verse 34: When God is present to people, sanctifying their depths, righteousness rolls down like an ever-flowing stream.

The love of God poured forth in our hearts by the Holy Spirit (Rom. 5:5) fulfills this Jeremiahan type. In Christian conviction, the Spirit given by Jesus to believers is the substance of the new covenant that Jeremiah foresaw. The Johannine church of the New Testament era was as convinced of this fact as the Pauline church. Indeed, verse 27 of the second chapter of First John seems directly indebted to Jeremiah, and it shows the primacy that the Johannine church long gave to individual conscience and the anointing of the Spirit. Only after considerable experience of the abuses to which an unbalanced stress on individual conscience could lead did the Johannine church submit itself to the hierarchical structure and other controls that were developing in what scholars sometimes call "the Great Church" of the pan-early-Christian community. And just as the Johannine church enriched the Great Church with a special appreciation of the divinity of Christ and the sacramentality of the Incarnation, so it brought a special appreciation of the graces, the intimate inner anointings, of the Spirit of the Word-made-flesh.

There are dozens of practical lessons in this Jeremiahan–Johannine appreciation of the primacy of God's inner workings, and I would not pretend to say which a given group of workers for peace and justice should find most helpful. I would say, though, that I find this biblical theology a sobering reminder that we will never get the peace and justice, the worldwide goodness, we long for and require until God works the genuine conversions that make the divine standards inner laws which people have no desire to violate. Just as the great artist works for the love and joy of it, so the great lover of God does what is right because the alternative has little attraction.

The saints do not feel compelled so much as privileged. Their prayer is as natural, as unquestioned, as their breathing, while their efforts to be useful to other people and succor the suffering express what they are more than what they have resolved. Even the rest of us, who sin and manifestly do not find self-sacrificing love obvious or easy, can feel that the Spirit is on our side. As well, we can think that what we and most other people most deeply want is the love of God, the divine beauty. In our hearts, God is laboring for peace and justice.

Why does Jeremiah feel the need to renew and interiorize the covenant?

How does Romans 5:5 relate to Jeremiah 31:33?

What is the ideal relationship between charismatic inspiration and peacemaking?

18

False Pastors

Ezekiel 34:1–12

Ezekiel, the third of the major Latter Prophets, writes out of the experience of exile. In his work we sense the psychic extremes to which a priestly spirit torn away from the Temple and the holy cult that had been the center of its life was driven. The wild imagery of Ezekiel reminds us that prophetic creativity, like many other species, can cost a great deal. The vision of the chariot recorded in Ezekiel 1 became a staple of Jewish mysticism, while the vision of the dry bones returned to flesh by the divine spirit (chapter 37) is one of the great types of the resurrection. On the other hand, Ezekiel's priestly sense that sin is a pollution and his expression of this sense in sexual imagery has been harmful for women and marriage. Ezekiel's other great symbol for Israel's defection, the false shepherding of its leaders, is more praiseworthy. It became a type for the depiction of Jesus as the Good Shepherd (John 10).

Using the formula consecrated by Israelite prophets, Ezekiel says that what he is going to unfold came to him as the word of the Lord. The implication is that it is less his own than the message of the Holy One of Israel. The phrase *son of man* here most likely means "very ordinary human being." Daniel 7 gives this title to a more celestial figure, while the use of the term in the synoptic Gospels shades both meanings. The word that Ezekiel is to prophesy is against the shepherds, the leaders, of Israel. The context makes it plain that the prophet thinks God holds them responsible for the Exile.

Ezekiel's basic charge is that the leaders have not labored for the welfare of the common people but have sought their own advantage. Verse 4 sounds like the exact opposite of the good service that the Lukan Jesus (4:18–19), drawing on Third Isaiah (61:1–2; 58:6), made the profile of his ministry. Through the mouth of Ezekiel, God writes up a withering brief: "The weak you have not strengthened, the sick you have not healed, the crippled you have not bound up, the strayed you have not brought back, the lost you have not sought, and with force and harshness you have ruled them."

The result of this neglect and mismanagement is that the sheep, the people of Israel, have been scattered and have become food for wild beasts. Because the kings, priests, and prophets of Israel have not done their job, because they have padded their own pockets rather than spent themselves for the common good, Israel is now a slave in exile. As verse 10 puts it, this dereliction of duty has turned the Lord God against the shepherds of Israel, and God will actively require (an accounting of) the sheep at their hand. Indeed, God will take the sheep away from the shepherds' charge and see that the sheep are no longer gouged. In verses 11–12 God promises to take charge of the sheep, seek them out, and rescue them from their scatteredness. The context of exile makes this promise a prediction of return to Jerusalem, while the general message, ringing down the ages, is that God has promised that divinity, and no lesser agency, will be the main guide of the chosen people (and of humanity at large).

This text cries out for application to present-day leadership. In both the churches and the nations, God is judging those who should be paving the way for peace and justice. And while the ultimate sentence that any particular leader deserves rests in the shadows of the divine mystery, our text more than justifies our looking at both religious and secular leaders with a critical eye. Quite clearly, it implies that the main criterion of good leadership in either realm is the flourishing of the people. As Karl Rahner, the distinguished Roman Catholic theologian, once put it, just as the leaders of a chess club exist only so that the members may play good chess, so the leaders of the church exist only for the good living of Christian life. Rahner was not, of course, placing the Body of Christ on the level of the local Knights and Pawns. But he was making the quite pragmatic and biblically sanctioned point that we can know the quality of any church leadership by the fruits of worship and social service it is producing.

This would seem to mean that people laboring for peace and justice ought to find in the leadership of their churches strong support and encouragement. It would seem to mean that when churches are slow to rally behind programs to advance disarmament, literacy, health care for the poor and the elderly, care for the environment, racial equality, sexual equality, and the like the leadership is ripe for accusation and change. When present-day bishops, priests, ministers, elders, and boards seem quite well rewarded for their pastoral labors, we ought to get suspicious and look sharply at the condition of the flock.

Jesus, we recall, came to minister, not to be ministered unto. Jesus and most of the saints wore themselves out for the sake of their charges. Fortunately, we can point to many religious leaders today, as in most other eras, who do walk in the footsteps of Jesus, the great rabbis, and the other religious saints. Fortunately, there are many situations in which the people to be commiserated and supported are the self-spending leaders, while the people to be castigated are the indolent, grass-munching flocks. But we still do not have the flourishing of the people, whether in the churches or in the nations at large, that one would expect a fully effective leadership to produce. We still do not have the full application of the members' talents to peace and justice that vital faith would produce. Therefore, there is still much to blame in the church.

All the more so does Ezekiel 34 suggest dire things about the quality of the secular leadership that one finds in both the United States and the other Northern nations. Recently, economists have added to their usual list of woes a pattern in the United States that, if continued, will soon make us a two-tiered society. The wealthy are becoming wealthier and more numerous. The poor are becoming poorer and more numerous. The middle class is becoming an endangered species. In the same line, while the coasts enjoy boom times, the middle of the country lags behind. The leadership seems quite content with these patterns, quite willing to recreate with the rich and cut more and more helps to the poor. The defense industries purr along, protected by an aggressive mythology that characterizes Communism as satanic. If one were to strip this mythology of its patina of patriotism and make it show its theological colors, it would clearly be revealed as a Manichean dualism of light and darkness, of goodness and evil, and so as heretical. But because few political scientists think theologically and too many powerful people are profiting handsomely, the Manicheanism goes little challenged.

A comprehensive critique of present leadership in the United States would indict the religious shepherds for not better defending the flock from the selfishness so often ravaging it. It would sound from many more pulpits and national offices than it has that the good life targeted by most of our advertising and much of our military and economic policy is by biblical standards trash. It would echo in many more family rooms and church community centers than it has that whether poor and sick people are helped or not helped, not charisma on television, is the basis on which leadership is to be judged.

The guillibility of the flocks in recent elections says that the pastors and teachers of our country have been woefully incompetent or ineffective. The capitulation to mammon and its minions should be enough to give anyone charged with religious leadership a great fit of fear and trembling. This kind of demon certainly calls for prayer and fasting, but it also calls for crisp intellectual assault. From policies in Central America to policies on farming and welfare, what I have seen recently is grossly idolatrous and antibiblical. God will certainly require of our recent leaders the sheep they have gouged, but all the rest of us should make the same requirement of them.

What are the present-day implications of Ezekiel's attacks on the false shepherds?

Could one say that leadership in the church exists only to facilitate worship and social justice?

What prophetic function ought church leaders in the United States to exercise regarding military and social policies?

19

Judgment

Amos 5:14–24

Amos is usually accounted the first of the prophets whose oracles were committed to writing. Although he came from Tekoa in Judah, Amos was active in the Northern Kingdom around 750 B.C.E. prior to its fall to Assyria. Our text occurs in the midst of various prophecies of coming punishment (3:1–6:14), and several of its images are deservedly famous. Let us contemplate these images and then consider their present-day relevance.

The counsel of verse 14 that Israel is to seek good that it may live reminds us of the Deuteronomic conviction that ethical behavior should bring flourishing (Deut. 30:19–20). The correlative truth, that unethical behavior should bring destruction, was vivid enough in the prophet's mind to make him fear for Israel's future. Note in verse 15 that Amos wants justice established in the gate, that is, the basic passageway through which people pass. (Often judgment on legal cases would be rendered at the city gates.) This prophet is one of the best examples of the biblical insistence that what people do is more important than what people say. He illustrates, as well, a counterbalance to the overconcern with cultic matters that the priestly ranks often displayed. For a prophet such as Amos, offering a sacrificial animal but not doing justice was inverted, disordered religion. Only when the people did what was right, only when they acted fairly and compassionately, could they expect their cult to please God.

Verses 16 and 17 anticipate sorry suffering as a punishment

for the injustice Israel has indulged. We cannot know whether Amos himself foresaw the fall of Israel to Assyria, but certainly the final editors of his materials were bound to see in them intuitions that the sufferings that came were instruments of God's chastisement. In indicating both farmers and vineyards, Amos is suggesting that the punishment will pervade all ranks.

Verse 18 again brings before us the day of the Lord—the time of judgment. Amos is famous for having charged this concept with darkness and foreboding. Whereas it might connote the time when God would liberate Israel and redress its sufferings, for Amos it first suggests divine reckoning with the evils of Israel itself. Liking the day to fleeing from a lion only to meet a bear makes this point dramatically. If things are bad now, think what they would be if God were to come to administer strict judgment! The same with the picture of going into one's house, feeling safe, and then being bitten by a serpent. Amos will not let Israel think God is its pawn or simpleminded protector. The sovereignty and holiness of his God force the prophet to remind Israel that the day of the Lord will mean the revelation of all its sins.

Verses 21–24 have established the prophet's reputation as more interested in justice than cult. He probably had no quarrel with traditional worship as long as it did not become a cloak for injustice, a way of avoiding the practical work for peace and right order that genuine Israelite faith entailed. So the God of Amos is said to hate the feasts and solemn assemblies of a people whose heart is not in the right place. The Lord takes no pleasure in sacrifices if the hearts of those sacrificing are not pure or if an agenda of unjust dealings rumbles forward. For God to accept sacrifices implied that God accepted the people offering themselves through the sacrificial gifts. That simply could not be, unless such people were honest to the point of expressing their religion through just relations with their neighbors. God is bound to find offensive song and dance that dishonestly cover up an unwillingness to carry out the ethical requirements of the covenant.

The punchline is verse 24, from which this book draws its title: "But let justice roll down like waters, and righteousness like an ever-flowing stream.'' To the mind of Amos, this is God's first desire. The songs and sacrifices are quite secondary. To the mind of Amos, people who do what is right, who intend justice, are bound to be pleasing to God, while the verdict is still out on people who sacrifice and sing and pray.

Certainly anyone who reads the Bible holistically will find no basis for writing the prophecy of Amos or Jesus into a bias against proper ritual and worship. It seems much more likely that both prophets assumed the legitimacy of Jewish cult and concerned themselves rather with abuses, disorders, and oversights. To their mind the ground-level concern was honesty and love practically shown. If a person loved God, that person inevitably would do right by the brother or sister who was at hand. One could not genuinely love God and lie to one's neighbor, cheat one's business partner, or be cold to the poor in one's city. God simply was not such an entity, such a reality. To love the real God, one was bound to feel compassion for the suffering. To honor the Holy One of Israel, one could only tell the truth. Consequently, not to feel compassion and tell the truth was to show through one's actions that one did not love the holy God. It was to flunk the most crucial test. Passing the test of singing well at the Sabbath service or offering a handsome monetary gift could not substitute for this more critical failure. First came righteousness and a desire for justice from the heart.

If we link this prophetic view of things with our prior reflection, we can see that pastors are as bound by the call to justice as ordinary people are. Leaders of the church and the nation may be judged by what policies they promote just as doctors, teachers, plumbers, and salespeople may. It is good for bishops and senators to show up in church and pray fervently, just as it is good for plumbers and teachers to do the same. The public profession of faith can be a benefit to any person and any community. But the bottom line remains what one does, where one's pushes and pulls on the economy, the recreational realm, the arts, and the political dealing and wheeling would send them.

We all know that religion suffers greatly when charges of hypocrisy against religious people seem well founded. And even when we rush to make a few distinctions, speaking up for the mysteries of conscience, the ultimacy of divine mercy, and the tangledness of most human beings' moral accounts, we have to admit that some of the greatest obstacles to the spread of the gospel come from the unconversions and the injustices carried out by people who go to church but act like pagans on the job. God hates the feasts of people like this. The God of Amos hates the solemn assemblies of people like us when, on the Fourth of July, Bicentennial Day, or the Centennary of the Statue of Liberty, we pretend to a justice and mercy that seem to me quite dubious. Neither our past history nor our present national policies give us grounds for boasting before the God of a prophet like Amos.

Our past history, to be sure, contains many things of which we may be proud—the guarantee of religious liberty and a new opportunity for many beleaguered people high among them. But when we look carefully at this past, blacks, other ethnic minorities, and women, to use the most obvious categories, have grounds for demur. Miners, factory workers, farm workers, domestic workers, and many others from the underside of the economy and culture stand as accusing angels, today even more than yesterday. Do the people who say the formal prayers in the great national churches really think that God forgets the children of Central America, or the mothers who stand vigil because their children have "disappeared"? Can the programs against drugs and for literacy blot out the poverty in the ghettoes and the low salaries in the schools? The deficits in the budgets that mortgage the future generations bespeak a blindness and self-serving that any real God has to assail. The expenditures for weapons of destruction, like the concern for paper fortunes made through useless mergers, shout that our leaders have made the flourishing of their whole flock a very low priority.

So let there be more talk about justice in our liturgical assemblies and less talk about our civil religion. Let there be sober recall that in 1776 only about 12 percent of the colonial population was listed on church rolls. By 1980, the church rolls in America were numbering about 62 percent of the population. Can we suppose that our country is now more upstanding and righteous than at that previous time?

Why did Amos shift the interpretation of the Day of the Lord from rescue to judgment?

What qualifications does Amos place around public worship?

What is the present state of justice regarding Central America, women in the United States, and blacks in the United States?

20

False Trust

Hosea 10:9–15

Like Amos, the prophet Hosea was active in the Northern Kingdom in the eighth century, prior to the conquest by Assyria. The fame of Hosea rests on the intimacy he found in the covenant between God and Israel. Like a wife who had proven unfaithful, Israel had spurned the love of a God who wanted to espouse it most tenderly. In this passage the prophet contemplates the sorry sufferings that strike him as Israel's just desserts. Because the people have trusted in weapons rather than in the love of their God, they shall reap destruction in battle.

According to Judges 19, Gibeah was the site of a repulsive sin, the raping to death of a concubine. No doubt, when the prophet searched his memory for a powerful image of abuse and wickedness, this event came to mind. From the outset of this text, then, Hosea means to indict Israel scathingly. One senses that the depth of his insight into the intimacy that God offered through the covenant produced such anger. Like many of the saints, whose appreciation of God's goodness caused them to hate sin passionately, Hosea thinks of Israel as a people long unworthy of what God has offered them.

The Christian church does well to think of itself in the same way, not letting the holiness it derives from the Spirit of God blind it to its own sinfulness. From the time of Peter and the other disciples who fled, Jesus has gotten from us followers much less than he deserves. In Corinth, Galatia, and Thessalonica, Paul found people who belonged to the Body of Christ but did not serve it as they ought. Eastern Christianity, Roman Catholic Christianity, Protestant Christianity, fundamentalist Christianity—all have scandals to remember. The Gibeah to which the historian of any of those traditions instinctively would return is a good reason to grow humble and ask God not to visit any of the churches with the punishments they deserve.

In verse 11 we receive the prophet's conviction that God in fact has been patient with Israel, not dealing it the harsh training it merited. Verse 12 suggests how such training will come in the future and why it may turn out to be a boon: "Sow for yourselves righteousness, reap the fruit of steadfast love; break up your fallow ground, for it is the time to seek the Lord, that he may come and rain salvation upon you." By putting themselves to the plow of religious fidelity, Hosea's compatriots may harvest a good conscience, the spiritual health of right order under God. They may take home the experience of God's steadfast love (the special epithet of the biblical God—constant warmth and helpfulness). The plots of talent, resources, faith, prayer, and the rest that people have not used can come into cultivation. A little effort, even some forced labor, may prove immensely beneficial. All this remains completely true today, when the majority of people who have tepid religious lives, like the majority of churches that are less than assemblies of God, would profit immensely from a simple infusion of discipline.

If today we are to hear such a prophetic word, we must seek the Lord through the biblical message. Taken to heart, the words of Hosea or Jesus can bridge our way to the Lord. They can break up the dry ground, make straight the path of consolation. Time past means less to God than time present. God can make all things new, and if we read Hosea as an expression of God's concern, of God's willingness to be angry rather than to write Israel off, God very much wants to make things new. Given a chance, seeing the door open, the Spirit of God would water the dry ground and make salvation bloom. What is salvation, in fact, but the healing, the reunion with God, that God's Spirit is in labor to effect?

A prophet such as Hosea lays on the lash, if that be the only way to get people's attention. He thinks that divinity itself lays on the lash, or at least allows people to reap the consequences of their follies, if that be the only way to bring them to their senses. Somehow we must realize that nothing but divinity, the sole Creator, is a sure reliance. Somehow the truth in the account of creation, that we have come from dust and depend on God for each breath we draw, has to take root. Hosea sees Israel on the brink of learning, to its sorrow, that it has been trusting in wretched, useless powers. He would rather see the people wracked by pain and so brought back to their senses than to see them continue in such ruinous stupidity.

The remainder of our text is all too relevant today, when the nations' trust in chariots and warriors makes the militarism of Israel look like a game of toy soldiers. We have grown little more mature than the Israel of 2750 years ago when it comes to the matter of how to orient ourselves in the universe. We still think that meaning and prosperity are to be found in power and the capacity to destroy those who oppose our will. We still do not know that the force that creates life, beauty, healing, and holiness is of a very different order.

The obvious reminders for peacemakers are right there in the text—a classical prophet has laid it out that one cannot serve war and God. But the less obvious lesson may be that peacemakers have to become mystagogues, people capable of indicating where God is in personal and national life. If we call for peace but do not know where to point people when they want the peace that the world cannot give, we are not living up to Hosea's example. If those who seek the Lord and ask about the experience of feeling salvation rain down find us embarrassed and mute, they will doubt that we know much beyond the religious slogans.

The prophet Hosea had learned about the marital love of God through the sufferings of his own unfortunate alliance. The parallel in so many other cases holds true: We speak effectively only about what we know personally, what we can describe from having been there. Have we been to the place where the still, small voice seems more persuasive than the cannons of war? Do we really know the alternatives to power plays and military buildups? The way to peace cannot be separated from the way to justice, beauty, and holiness. The love on which children depend for their health indicates the same God as the love that forgives one's enemies. God must become so simple, deep, and real a love that God is everywhere and omnirelevant. At least as our ideal, we must know a trust in God like the trust that Hosea had learned, a reliance strong enough to make the engines of war seem immature, crude, and retarded.

But just where are we to gain such conviction and experience? Just how might it come? There is no indication that Hosea or the other prophets bought their blazing faith at some secret black market. True enough, they may have belonged to prophetic schools that trained them in faith and eloquence, but we have no evidence that such schools were esoteric, elitist, or focused on special disciplines. The greater likelihood, especially in the case of Hosea, whose work brims with autobiographical suggestions, is that the prophets stood between their given family circumstances and the mystery of their God, trying their best to make the two connect. Always it was a question of how what they were experiencing illumined the nature of their God and a question as well of how what they believed about God illumined what they were experiencing. If God was as the covenants claimed, then Hosea could believe that his tattered marriage still might prove redemptive. If his marriage was any clue to the nature of the divine love, then Israel was sure to suffer for abandoning its spouse and relying on chariots and warriors.

For ourselves, things remain much the same. If God is as the face and voice of Christ suggest, then nothing in our family lives or our jobs can be a final deadend. If what makes for peace in the home and creativity at work is an indication of how God wants to move in the wider world, then governmental policies that promote strife, confrontation, and escalation of rhetoric and violence are foolishness pure and simple. The prophet would have us proceed very differently, first sowing righteousness.

Illustrate how God's patience has worked in your own life.

How do our nation and our church show they continue to rely more on riches and power than on the true God?

How does the love which children most need relate to the love responsible for creation?

III

Writings

The Wisdom Inculcated by Oppression and the Divine Silence

21

The Law

Psalm 1:1–6

The third collection of scriptural writings in our present Old Testament had gained its authoritative status by the end of the first century C.E. Many of the individual pieces, however, had been revered for centuries. Indeed, in the case of some of the psalms, we find prayers, bits of poetry, and lyrics that probably go back to the united monarchy of David and Solomon (tenth century B.C.E.). The association of psalms with the official cult of the Temple suggests that priestly authors probably played a large role, but we learn from such late historical works as Ezra, Nehemiah, and Chronicles that most of Israel's spiritual reforms entailed a reinvigoration of official worship and so involved rulers and prophets as well as priests.

Psalm 1, which we have to assume owes its position to a deliberate choice on the part of the final editors, is usually classified as a wisdom psalm. The love of the Torah, the Law, that the psalm expresses is characteristic of the wisdom writers. To delight in the law of God and meditate upon it day and night became the ideal of rabbinic spirituality. Other sapiential writings stress the counsel of God that moves the stars and the seas, but the Torah our present text has in mind most likely is the law of Moses. In addition, we sense the Deuteronomic conviction that following the Torah will bring prosperity while wickedly violating the Torah will bring doom.

To be blessed, in biblical parlance, is to feel God's favor.

Most of the biblical authors think of this favor as something quite concrete. Their instinctive image is not of a tidy account, pleasing to God the great banker. Rather it is of fruitfulness, productiveness, good health, and rich bounty. The tree planted by the stream is well watered. The person who follows the Torah can expect healthy children, good business dealings, and many reasons to bless both sunrise and sunset.

For the moment we can bracket the question of what happens to faith like that of Psalm 1 when people keep faith with the Torah and still experience suffering. Here we can linger with the praiseworthy biblical instinct that staying close to God, following the divine will and counsel, ought to bring an all-around human prospering. The other side of this instinct, equally apparent in the psalm, is that violating God's ordinances ought to bring one to punishment and ruin. The wicked, by the psalm's own imagery, ought to be like chaff driven by the wind. By the end of the psalm, it is true, justice has been reserved to God. God knows the way of the righteous, and presumably God will (somehow) reward the righteous as they deserve. The way of the wicked, whom God also knows, will cause them to perish (at the hand of God, if not in this-worldly terms). The psalmist cannot conceive of God blessing the way of the wicked; and, because all prosperity finally comes from God, any prosperity the wicked seem to enjoy must be false or merely provisional.

One could easily reflect that studying and following the Torah of God eventually become their own reward, as rabbis and theologians have often concluded. If we are sufficiently spiritual to find our primary nourishment in contemplation of the divine beauty and justice, our fortunes in the world of business and social reputation become quite secondary. But neither the Old Testament nor the New Testament pushes this spiritualism without limitation. Certainly both make it plain that God is the prime treasure for which the human heart has been made, so that even when wealth, reputation, and health wither people can still experience peace and joy. But neither testament admits a division between body and spirit, nature and God, or decent material circumstances and spiritual joy that would make creation or history unimportant.

The biblical God is the source of a natural beauty and power which ought, on the whole, to provide human beings a healthy and happy life. The covenants of the biblical God intend the flourishing of a people who astound outsiders by the love they show one another and the rich measures of mutual respect and support they give to one another. Biblical religion considers suffering abnormal and a sign that creatures have tampered with God's plan. However frequent, indeed commonplace, suffering turns out to be, it always remains a negative index. To be sure, God proves so good and creative that God finds a way to redeem even suffering. The cross of Christ, for example, is the pathway to Paul's new creation. But in our work for peace and justice we need to make it clear that the sufferings and disorders of warmaking are out of joint with what devotion to God's Torah ought to bring. Equally, we need to make it clear that famine, illiteracy, infant mortality, and the many other effects of worldwide poverty stand cursed by God as opposed to God's creative will.

The classical modern foes of religion, such as Feuerbach, Marx, Nietzsche, and Freud, got great mileage from the fact that many adherents of religion in their time had given up this positive view of God's intentions. For many wealthy churchgoers, God had put the goods of creation into the hands of those best able to administer them, and what happened to the many poor peasants or industrial workers was something that God would take care of on Judgment Day. At the turn of the present century, wealth and power were signs that God had elected certain people to positions of trust, and so such people could feel quite good about their heavenly prospects.

For many poor people, the sufferings of earthly life either completely discredited the notion of a just God or removed the reality of such a God to a heavenly realm that had no connection with work and family life here below. Religion, therefore, could be an opiate, drugging people against the pains of daily life in industrial Europe. It could be used by those enjoying power and wealth to prop the status quo. Indeed, in the most pernicious of cases the powerful could claim that the poor were suffering because of the disfavor of God and so must be sinners.

The clear veto on these modes of thinking lay as near as the pages of the synoptic Gospels, of course; and one can only think that the failure of many modern people to perceive the discrepancy between their Christian faith and the teachings of Jesus stemmed from a strong desire not to know. The Sermon on the Mount tells any with ears to hear that God blesses people by a different standard than their bank accounts.

How to reconcile such a synoptic beatification with what Psalm 1 has in mind is a considerable question, of course, but we cannot lay down either conviction. God has to want the flourishing of those who follow the divine law and has to be creative enough to find ways to compensate those who follow but still suffer. If we say that God does not want a beautiful creation and a healthy covenanted people, we have made the divinity sadistic. If we say that the judgments of God are the judgments of our accountants and the editors of our society pages, we have canonized the awful injustices of secular culture. The only solution, it seems, is to develop a faith sophisticated enough to be able to say several things simultaneously.

First, God must hate the nations' warmongering and economic injustices, since these so blight creation and spawn human misery. A good creator has to want the health and happiness of her children. Second, God must stand by those who follow the divine standards, the Torah of truth and love, at cost, at least occasionally making it a matter of inner experience that meditating on this Torah, praying with whole mind-heart-soul-and-strength, brings an unequaled peace and joy. Third, in the person of Jesus, God has shown what divinity is doing about the evils that human beings carry out and suffer. God has shown that divinity does not stand aloof from misery and injustice but spends itself succoring them. Indeed, Jesus on the cross says that God has taken the full brunt of human wickedness to heart and let the Christ suffer it unto death. The resurrection of Jesus, which is also the resurrection of human hopes, is no cheap grace but rather the most costly expression of the divine creativity.

Describe the joy of meditating on God's law day and night.

How are famine and illiteracy illumined by God's law?

Why is it especially pernicious to say that the sufferings of the poor are a punishment of God?

22

Forsakenness

Psalm 22:1–11

It is a commonplace saying that the psalter has something for every mood and situation. If we want to praise God purely for the simple splendor of the divine goodness, we can go to Psalm 150. If we want an expression of abandonment, of feeling forsaken and turning to God as our last resort, we can go to Psalm 22. For the evangelists, Jesus, brought by his passion into the darkest of moods, went to Psalm 22 and came away able to surrender his spirit into the hands of his divine Father. The implication might be that any of us feeling abandoned or discouraged can take our pain to God and hope to be helped.

When are we liable to feel that God has abandoned us? When we find other human beings and secular events ranged against us, of course, but also when our spirits are fatigued and desolate. Long before pastoral theology had enlisted the help of clinical psychology, people interested in the spiritual life had observed that wisdom seems to cut a path between two suspicious extremes. The first suspicious extreme is euphoria—feeling so good, so graced, that everything looks easy. The problem here is overconfidence. Beginners, especially, can forget that without the grace of God they are nothing. The second suspicious extreme is depression that paints everything black. The problem here is that nothing looks possible. Even people of middle age and considerable experience can forget that human weakness is not the measure of God's ability to save.

The voice of Psalm 22 comes from the depths of negativity. God seems far away, careless, and silent. Note in verse 2 the revealing confession that the petitioner can find no rest. Life has lost its sabbatical, gracious character. Overwork and overstrain have robbed the person of peace. The lesson would seem to be that the person ought to ease away from the excessive care that might be contributing to the sense of hopelessness. And even if there is no excessive care, even if the person has no freedom and is doing well just to endure assaults beyond his or her control, the counsel could be to hand it over to God, to make one's petitions and then let happen what will.

In verses 3–5 we find reasons for thinking that the silent God may in fact give a word and spring into action. That happened in the past, above all in the Exodus. Therefore, it could happen in the present. The Christian parallel would be the recall of Christ's passion and resurrection, which of course form the axis of each celebration of the Lord's Supper. Nothing could be blacker than the death of God's holy messenger, and yet it is the very marrow of Christian faith that God proved more powerful than death, raising the messenger into the divine deathlessness.

Verses 6–8 are touching in their self-centeredness, and they legitimate our own going to God with frank outpourings of how humiliated and defeated we feel. The posture of truly honest prayer includes this frankness, this emotional outpouring. If we think that we can pray to God only when we look like an ad for perfect grooming, we know little about biblical religion. We rather should let God know the bitterness and gall we taste, the shame that humiliates us. If we can acknowledge this, get it out and objectify it, God can begin healing us. If we can tax God with responsibility to save us from such real, wracking trials, God may finally become experiential.

The final verses of our text express a second movement of trust. The psalmist recalls further titles by which God can be considered eager and dependable to help. Without God, there would have been no birth, no life, no upbringing by mother and father. From the beginning, God has been the one resource, the sole rock and salvation, to whom the psalmist has been entrusted. So in a profound sense the current troubles merely have crystallized the primacy of God that the psalmist was taught long ago: When there is no one to help, God can turn out to be close as a thought, as near as a sigh.

How does all this relate to people made weary by the trials of peacemaking, to people heartsick at the persistence of poverty and injustice? It reminds us of the mystery of God's ways and of the depths to which religious fidelity may force us. By the statistics that the newspapers and the government bureaus provide, there is no reason to think that peace is drawing near. Equally, there is no reason to think that suffering is on the decrease and poverty is winding down. So we have to go beyond the horizon of the newspapers and the government bureaus, venturing out into the realm of the Spirit.

The Spirit, it seems, does not accept its definition of what is possible from the pundits of Capitol Hill. The Christ did not evaluate success and failure in terms of what happened to the gross national product or the Dow Jones industrials. For Jesus it was enough to speak today the good news that God poured into his heart, to extend here and now what healing and help the Father and the Spirit made possible. Jesus knew that people had to open themselves to him if he was going to heal them. He knew that for his words to be taken as good news people had to be longing for liberation. But he did what he could, seizing the few days God gave him, and so when he gave over his spirit he could feel consummated.

The psalmist combats desolation and abandonment by crying out to God. By the simple fact of giving voice to such pain, the psalmist opens the wound to healing. God stands in the universe of the psalmist as the counter to absurdity, pain, and defeat. Despite all of the mystery in the name *God* it keeps hopelessness at bay. How much worse off are those who can see nothing in the curve of population growth but millions more starving children. That the forsakenness of such people must be nearly unbearable is probably why distraction and superficiality so often beguile them.

The great enemy of peacemaking, of radical politics intent

on a new economic justice, and of help for the poor is precisely the distraction of people who might make a solid contribution. No doubt such people are quite shaped by disillusionment, if not despair, but were they to face what they were feeling the Spirit might lance their boils. God, peace, and justice seldom lose by people growing reflective, critical, or prayerful. With any providential nod, reflection, criticism, and prayer break open the assumptions with which we begin and force us to say that we do not know; things might change, and there could be other scenarios than the few we now can imagine. But until we do turn to God, until we are willing to face our pains and frustrations, cynicism and despair can have an easy time of it. Until our political action is informed by a deep contemplation, our commitment is quite in peril.

What kept Jesus to his commitment? Surely it was not the comeliness of the crowds or the suavity of the disciples. True, Jesus had his successes with the crowds, and there is no reason to whittle down the satisfaction that living professions of faith brought him. But the evangelists make it plain that Jesus had many reasons for calling Psalm 22 to mind. Before he was arrested and brought to his death, he already sensed that the prevailing powers had turned against him. So Jesus kept going because he had found a will, a mission, a love that meant more to him than either saving his skin or gaining this-worldly success. He kept going because he felt the Father asked him to keep going and the welfare of those around him made it imperative.

We need to abandon our lesser motives for peacemaking and social justice before they abandon us. As soon as God invites us, we need to face the darkness of likely failure and cry out to God our hurt. Jesus was not pretty at his finale. He was defeated and ridiculed. So if we find ourselves defeated and ridiculed, we can think ourselves in good company. If we find ourselves thinking God has abandoned us, we can be at the beginning of real prayer. For God, darkness and light, failure and success are still to be determined. Right now is never the end.

What does Psalm 22 teach us about the silence of God?

What can one properly say to people who feel abandoned by God?

What does Jesus' use of Psalm 22 during his crucifixion suggest about his sense of abandonment?

23

Worship

Psalm 99:1–9

This psalm reminds us that Israel thought of God as its king. The first verse establishes that God is king of the universe, maker of heaven and earth, awesome power before whom all that breathes should bow. The second verse depicts God as established, enthroned, in Zion, on the holy hill of Jerusalem that Israel considered the center of the world. It is no accident that this hill was the site of the Temple and so the center of the Israelite cult.

The next three verses praise God's holiness. God's name is great, even terrible. God loves justice and establishes equity. Therefore the people should worship the Lord, should pour forth their praise, their adoration, their confession that they owe God their entire being. In the past, God has heard the cries of the people and accepted the services of their priests. Since worship has been pleasing, God has kept intimacy as in the wilderness, regularly visiting the people in the pillar of fire and cloud. Verse 7 reminds the psalmist's readers that Moses, Aaron, Samuel, and the other paragons of priestly worship kept the statutes of the Lord. They could approach the Holy One with clean hands. In verses 8 and 9 the implications for the present stand clear: God might be responsive and forgiving today, as in the past. God might champion the people and avenge the evils they have suffered. The part of the people is to worship their God and so give the divine holiness its due.

Today worship presents different problems. The cosmological

foundations for awe before the divine power have shifted. People who know about the frontiers of research in astrophysics, molecular biology, and similar fields certainly have reason to bow low before the profusion of the divine creativity, but ordinary people seldom experience the raw shock of an earthquake or a flood that would remind them how small they are. Moreover, we tend to think of holiness in moral rather than physical terms. The power of a nuclear explosion certainly can take our breath away, but we don't instinctively regard that power as holy.

Worship, to be sure, has always been fired by the creature's awe at the power of the divine Creator. Yet for biblical religion this power has not been the theological crux. Rather it is the goodness of God, the holiness that shows in the divine compassion, that biblical worship has spotlighted. In the Christian case, it is the prodigality of the divine love revealed through Christ on the cross. Christians certainly want to praise the Creator who transcends all physical powers, standing prior to any big bang and waiting beyond all entropy. But they want to praise more the Father who so loved the world that he gave the only begotten Son, the Son who did not call them servants but friends, and the Spirit poured forth in their hearts for divinization.

This moral transcendence of God glimmers in the parables that Jesus used to depict his Father and the kingdom. The son who is prodigal in selfishness (Luke 15) learns that his father is prodigal in selflessness, caring only that the son return to himself and prosper. The elder son strikes us as prodigal in stupidity: How could he have lived so long in the presence of such a father and learned so little? The parable about the man who hires workers at different hours throughout the day and at the end gives them all equal pay points in the same direction. God is so much better than we are, so far beyond our calculations of rights and duties, that we have to strain even to get God in our sights. Jesus spoke of the sun that shines and the rain that falls on just and unjust alike. He spoke of the shepherd who leaves the ninety-nine sheep that are safe to search for the one sheep that is lost. He spoke of the woman who sweeps her house in search of the single coin that is missing. Both the lilies of the field and the birds of the air receive from God what they need. If we, evil as we are, still manage to do good to our children, how much better must God want to do?

To Jesus' mind, one could not trust God excessively. God stood beyond all pettiness, all desire for revenge, all justice in a narrow or vindictive sense. God need never have created the world. For anything to be was an expression of the divine generosity. Even less need God have expended energy on saving the world. Yet God no more could abandon human beings than a nursing mother could abandon her child. Jesus himself no more could abandon his people or Jerusalem than he could curse the God whose love filled his heart.

When the Son of God went to his death neither defending himself nor cursing his enemies, the holiness of the deity became almost shocking. Could it be that God would suffer human evil, would undergo even death on the behalf of human beings? The logic of the death and resurrection of Christ takes us far beyond where we usually live. In most of our neighborhoods, God is not real enough and holiness is not significant enough to give us a fix on what God is about. For the fact is that Jesus lived for his Father in such a way that his core, what he most essentially was, never came into the possession of his enemies.

The Gospel of John shows the greatest appreciation of this fact, and in John 14–17 we find Jesus conversing with God as though he were already in heaven. When Jesus dies on the cross, John speaks of an hour long anticipated. At one level it is the hour of darkness, when Satan and the worst of human instinct triumph. At the higher level of divine interpretation, however, it is the hour of victory, when the love of the Son for the Father brings back to the Father a humanity capable of becoming divine. The death of Christ defeats death and takes human flesh into the divine deathlessness. The resurrection and outpouring of the Spirit are but the inevitable expression of this change of state. Death could not keep its hold on Jesus because the core of Jesus was strictly divine.

In such a perspective, what happens in the world of space and time takes on quite a new significance. The innermost meaning of any person's death is the yes or no to the divine mystery which it expresses. The final meaning of work for war or for peace is the testimony of unbelief or faith that it bears. When people spend themselves for justice, trying to make the world a place fit for images of God to live in, they keep the light of God shining in the darkness. Ultimately, the only crucial triumph is that this light not fail. When people go beyond the letter of the law and pour compassion on the wounds of those who suffer, they keep the love of God credible. That, too, is the crucial triumph. The symbols of Christian faith deal in divine realities—deathlessness, goodness too pure to retaliate, truth so bright that for us it must be a cloud of unknowing that we can glimpse only occasionally. The efforts we make at worship, like the efforts we make when we help other people for no personal gain, are certainly minimal, yet God is so good that God makes them suffice.

For Paul, life had changed so radically that the only thing he found important was Christ's living in him. For saints of all stripes, something similar has happened. The grace of God would bear all of us away from worldly strife into the beauty of a goodness that cannot fail. Just as Jesus was the Word who took flesh and dwelt among us, ultimately to bear the sins of our world, so are we, the branches of Jesus' vine, encouraged by the Spirit to love the divine beauty in the world, making our heavenly peace and joy fruitful for the poor and suffering. We cannot place peacemaking and struggling for justice in their proper contexts until we make them sacraments of heavenly life. If we will, they can suffuse the Spirit of the resurrected Lord.

Why was Israelite worship so shaped by a need to feel awe?

How does the prayer of Jesus reflect his great trust in God?

How could the divine goodness, too pure to retaliate, reset most discussions of peace and justice?

24

The Silence of God

Job 24:1–12

Scholars debate the date of the Book of Job. Many think that, although parts of the work may predate the Exile, the crucial composition occurred after 586 B.C.E., when Israel would have had special reason to ponder the divine justice. Our text comes from one of Job's speeches in response to the dubious comforts offered him by his friends. The friends take the Deuteronomistic tack that punishment bespeaks misdeeds. Job protests his innocence and challenges the assumption that God runs a tidy ship on which the good are rightly rewarded and the evil are rightly punished.

Verse 1 sounds the note of skepticism: If God is the great judge, why is it that God does not keep hours when people can go to have their rights and wrongs sorted out? Why do the people who pray to God or think they know God through the Torah never experience the revelation of God's justice and rule? Verses 2–4 exemplify the injustices that regularly cry out for redress. The fatherless, the widow, and the poor again and again need a champion, a defender, and where is God? Verses 5–8 seem to switch from evildoers and depict how the poor are forced to live—no better than wild beasts. Where the wicked prosper and have fertile vineyards, the poor are lucky to have the right to glean. Verse 9 shows the depths of depravity that God seems to countenance: Children are taken in payment of debts and set for forced labor.

Verses 10–11 paint still another picture of poor people laboring for the welfare of others, having no alternatives to practical slavery. The final verse of our text, verse 12, has the groans of the dying and the wounded rising to God, begging the divinity for aid. Yet God seems silent, paying no attention to their prayers. The drift of Job's argument is that talk of the divine justice is nugatory. If one is willing to honor the evidence of one's senses, God does little to punish the wicked or reward the virtuous for their sufferings.

By the end of the Book of Job this position will have been seriously questioned, and the counterquestion—Can any creature judge the Creator?—will have been put most strongly. Yet the authors of Job clearly labor to make the main character attractive, and we wonder even at the end whether Job has not had the better of the argument. On its own terms, with few indications that divinity is involved in the sufferings of the innocent and with no indications that divinity itself suffers from the evils that creation contains, the Book of Job is not persuasive that God cares about justice and ensures that righteousness wins out. The silence of God is too pervasive, the mismatch between evil and prospering is too great, for the friends of Job to convince us that we are involved in a process fully wise and holy.

One problem with the Book of Job is that its horizon is this-worldly. For Job the grave is the end of human existence, and what has not been recompensed by the grave remains never requited. The advantage of this position is that those who hold it cannot fly from this-worldly responsibilities. They must make their own conviction and their God bear on the here and now, on joys and sorrows sharpened by human mortality. The limitation of this position is that it does not let God be God. Perhaps God, who is not mortal, has ways of dealing with mortal joys and sorrows that take them beyond themselves. Perhaps God intends to wipe every tear from the eyes of those who suffer innocently on a day when death will be no more.

The New Testament gives numerous warrants for such thinking, so that by the time they come in the Book of Revelation they seem logical. At the time of the Book of Job Israel still had not probed the divine nature sufficiently to think in terms of immortality and deathlessness. Resurrection, the symbol that later Jewish thought would fashion, still hadn't come into force. Therefore, we must put brackets around many of Job's arguments. The conclusion they reach is valid enough if we accept their this-worldly premises, but their premises are less than certain.

The call to peacemaking and justice gains its urgency from the cries of those who suffer from warmaking and injustice. According to Job, "God pays no attention to their prayer." Is this true? How would we know? What follows if we in fact cannot know? These are some of the questions it would seem good for us to ponder.

How does God attend to our prayers? Jesus himself seems to depict prayer on the model of a conversation. Clearly, Jesus encourages people to pour out their troubles to God and to expect that God will respond. The disciples are to pray and never give up. They are to assume that God is on their side, interested in them, willing and able to give them help. But we notice that Jesus' own prayer in the Garden of Gethsemane did not receive the answer that, on the face of things, it sought. The cup did not pass from Jesus, so the will that was done was the Father's more than Jesus' human will. But if Jesus left the garden composed in spirit, peaceful enough to endure what he had to endure, was his prayer not answered? If he proved able to surrender himself to things he could not control, had not the Spirit strengthened him? In the aftermath of the death and resurrection of Jesus, the disciples thought the entire drama the providential unfolding of God's plan. So Luke, especially, speaks of the necessity of Jesus' suffering, and the disciples who encounter Jesus on the road to Emmaus have their eyes opened to God's purposes in Jesus' death.

I see no way that any of us can know with certainty whether people who cry out their pains to God have their cries answered. This means that we should neither promise glibly that God supports the poor and the suffering nor take at face value the signs that such people lead utterly wretched lives.

It seems to me legitimate to charge God with the responsibility of justifying each person's existence. A life in which a person had no chance at peace, joy, and significance would seem unworthy of God. But what can count for significance and how peace and joy can come fall outside my competence.

I cannot say that parents forced to watch their children starve or turn into addicts or be sexually abused have other experiences which justify their lives or even their parenthood. I cannot explain why God should require such sufferings or how God is acquitted of the charge of most unholy cruelty. On the other hand, I also cannot say for certain that God has no means of self-acquittal or that parents who watch their children be ruined cannot still find reason to bless their Creator.

The simple fact is that none of us knows in these matters. Are we to weigh more heavily the shabby tenement, grimy with the despair of the worst barrio, or the flower still exhibited at the window? Do the tumbledown bricks and the stains of blood count for more or less than the cloudless blue sky? People have to choose what weights the different factors in their lives are to have, and we have to grant the Spirit the freedom to deal with each person individually.

As long as peace remains a possibility and justice is not a complete chimera, the followers of Jesus and biblical religion have enough to keep them going. As long as acid rain has not taken away all blue skies and child abuse is not intrinsic to parenting, the enemies we must combat are still manageable. God's job, we might say, is to keep the future open. God must provide enough answers to prayers, enough healing of broken spirits and bodies, to make prayer and therapy seem worthwhile. Beyond that, each person has the right, indeed the privilege, of finding God unique. The mysteriousness of each person's relationship with God and of each person's sense of the justice that life has or has not afforded and the challenge that death presents keeps religion open as a viable option. No defender of religion should ask people to falsify their testimony or water down the threats to meaning they find in human suffering, but neither should any proponent of atheism or any debunker of religion be allowed to claim full knowledge of what suffering or joy implies. All of us finally are silenced and humbled, as Job in fact finally was. Each of us must trust that God pays attention.

What evidence does Job have on his side when he challenges the silence and justice of God?

How can we trust that God answers the prayers of the wretched—or the prayers that we ourselves would most like to make?

How strongly should we weigh the mystery that beauty does flash forth, that love does occur, that now and then enemies are reconciled?

25

The Champion

Job 29:7–17

Job certainly stands in the biblical collection of personalities as the one who most directly questions the justice of God. But it is noteworthy that Job also presents one of the best biblical descriptions of justice. Chapter 29 is famous for the high-minded ethics that it describes, and in these verses that we are considering Job emerges as a great champion of the poor and downtrodden, a great fighter for justice. Of course, this only makes the challenge to God the sharper, for, if Job, a mere human being, can spend himself so fully on behalf of the suffering, how can God remain silent?

We notice, first, that Job is recalling a time prior to his misfortunes when he had great status in his community. Verses 7–8 depict a man of eminence in whose presence others cede primacy and honor. Both the young and the aged honored Job then. His prosperity and his wisdom won him respect all around. Even princes grew still and listened for his counsel. Even nobles feared that by babbling they would miss a shaft of light. Verse 11 claims that Job's virtue was clear to all who heard or saw him. He was a public figure well approved by his public deeds. So the first part of the profile that Job claims amounts to a fine reputation. Ask any of his contemporaries and they would have hastened to describe him as a pillar of his community.

With verse 12 the profile of Job becomes even more impressive. Job claims that he delivered the poor and helped the fatherless. His own substance was sufficient for him to aid those in want. His sense of paternal responsibility and care led him to extend his family and concern himself with the orphaned. He saved many who were about to perish and so won for himself their blessing. Widows whose lives were heavy with grief came to think of his presence as cause for joy. Verse 14 is a very proud claim, so proud in fact that if it were not true Job would be a thorough hypocrite: "I put on righteousness, and it clothed me; my justice was like a robe and a turban." One cannot go much further than this in Old Testament terms. The blessing of the Israelite God clearly was upon people of wealth and honor who extended themselves for their community and championed the poor.

The further claims that Job makes in verses 15–17 only fill out this portrait. He does not suggest that he was able to heal the blind or the lame, but he does claim that he gave them all the help he could. He does not claim that he was able to eliminate the poverty of the most lowly or to right the cause of all who needed help, but he does claim that he made their concerns his own. And, in the last verse of our text, Job even claims to have fought actively against the unrighteous, inflicting penalties on them and forcing them to let go of their prey. So here we have a great champion of what was right, a great defender of the defenseless, brought low for no apparent reason. By the canons of the Deuteronomic theology Job should have reaped from God only continued prosperity. Clearly, therefore, something was wrong with this theology.

We see much of what was wrong with the Deuteronomic theology when we contrast the portrait of Job with the portrait of Jesus. Deuteronomy was wise to require that God always be the defender of justice, the upholder of those who keep to the paths of righteousness, but it tended to conceive of such divine defense in rather narrow terms. Because the basic horizon of Deuteronomic theology was the small span of years that mortal human beings could enjoy, that theology felt pressured to make God a source of this-worldly bounty for the good and a source of this-worldly punishment for the wicked. So a person like Job, who did all that the Torah could ask and yet went from prosperity to misery, brought Deuteronomic theology into crisis. People who labored for peace and justice ought to have experienced not only peace and justice but also material abundance. Second Isaiah realized that the justice of God might be considerably more profound than that, but without the horizon of resurrection that broke open in the drama of Jesus of Nazareth such a profundity had few historical, experiential warrants.

We notice, then, that while Jesus certainly championed the poor as Job had done—indeed, Jesus is presented as able to heal the blind and the lame—he never enjoyed the material prosperity that Job enjoyed, and his reputation in the community was more ambiguous. Saying this does not diminish Job so much as it forces us to look more sharply at Jesus. First, Jesus seems more identified with the *anawim,* the poor people of the land, than with the financial, political, or religious establishment. When he is described as coming from Nazareth, we should hear in the description overtones of contempt—he is a rustic, a bumpkin. Nothing significant was likely to come from Nazareth. Jerusalem was the place to be from, the center of most of the action.

Second, Jesus had a mixed reputation, enjoying great favor with the common people, especially those who had seen him work cures, but increasingly alienating the Jewish establishment. As the evangelists describe it, Jesus was a stumbling block even before his scandalous death on the cross. The works he was doing forced people to reconsider their understanding of Torah. The message he was preaching called into doubt the proprieties of many established ways. Those who had a great deal invested in the prevailing orthodoxy, the prevailing ideology, tended to dismiss his works and words as extremely inconvenient. In the minds of the evangelists, these people fled the light that Jesus cast because their own deeds were evil. Because they did not really seek the will of God, the truth of God, the kingdom of God, they rejected God's Word made flesh.

Third, we also noticed that Jesus suffered innocently—at least as innocently as Job—and that even in his suffering he blessed God with his every breath. Jesus seems always to have assumed the justice that Job doubted. Even when Jesus uses the words of Psalm 22 to cry out his distress, we get the impression that these words are mainly a way for him to place himself in his Father's keeping. Jesus simply does not doubt that God will take better care of him than he could ever take of himself. Every indication is that Jesus believes that the growth of the kingdom is God's business even more than his own and that God will surely take care of such matters.

So the one whom Christians consider the greatest champion of peace and justice primarily concerns himself with stirring up people's trust in God. If people will repent of their present faithlessness and believe in the good news that God is knocking on the door asking to be let in to gift them with grace, they will experience what the reign of God might be like. If people will let the Spirit of God take over their lives, they will learn from the inside in indubitable ways why the nonviolent, forgiving ethic of Jesus is the only one consonant with the kingdom and the Father. God is so good that those who live God's life are bound to be good by God's model. Even when believers fail, the Spirit of God who restores them to health resets their bones in the conviction that love is the only force creative enough, powerful enough, delicate enough to make a world fit to live in.

Job remains completely admirable, defending the poor and giving help wherever he can. But Jesus reveals quite a new and more profound order, one in which God identifies with the poor and the victims of injustice, making their cause God's own. The great challenge to the justice of God latent in the problems of war and poverty finds in Job an eloquent spokesman. In Jesus the challenge is taken to a higher level where it appears that throughout God has been at work in the problems of war and poverty insinuating their solution. The solution to war is loving our enemies and doing good to those who persecute us. The solution to injustice and poverty is conceiving of humanity as the body of Christ, as an organic unity in which there is little mine and thine, in which the goods of the earth are fairly developed and distributed to all of the earth's people. We may not like these solutions, but Jesus continues to preach them.

How adequate is Job's sketch of the just person?

What is the evidence that Jesus conceived of the reign of God as bringing physical healing and justice?

How important is the innocence of Jesus, and what analogies does it bear to the sufferings of the poor in the third world, the sufferings of people penalized for their sex or color, and the sufferings of aborted children?

26

Righteousness

Job 31:1–40

In chapter 31 Job only enriches the portrait of ethical righteousness that we saw sketched in chapter 29. Here he virtually challenges God to find fault with him, claiming that in all ways he so feared the divine judgments that he took pains to do every good work required of him. Many of these good works we have already seen—he showed concern for the orphan and the widow, defended the poor, helped the suffering. Others are prescribed by biblical law, reminding us that Deuteronomy, Leviticus, and the other books that laid out Israel's ethical ideals sketched a very high standard. New in this chapter is Job's claim to sexual purity, and one interested in the relationship between social ethics and sexual propriety might reflect that a healthy sexual propriety makes for justice at the most intimate level, at the fusion of the humanity that God made male and female.

Still, today's reader of Job 31 finds something missing. If the reader is Christian, that something may be the victimhood of Jesus—his closer identification with those who suffer. But even if the reader is not Christian, the realization may come home that what Job describes is too private, too little concerned with social patterns and institutional structures. Today we should be more aware of what Reinhold Niebuhr saw when he spoke of "moral man and immoral society." Society is more than the sum of individual citizens, many of whom are quite virtuous in their private lives. Society is also the systems, the institutions, that citizens have erected to accomplish such major tasks as educating the young; healing the sick; and providing food, clothing, and services. The ways that we pay our taxes, defend our borders, elect our leaders, care for our elderly, and provide for our poor, all shape the quality of the life that we experience and thus help to determine whether we feel we are treated justly or unjustly. The priorities our leaders set, in which we conspire through our votes, have at least an equal weight.

Today social life is so complicated that good people can find themselves stockholders in dubious corporations; compassionate people can find themselves electors of leaders who make life harder on the poor. Few theologians, certainly, are going to be competent to make all the distinctions that social ethics now require, but all theologians have the obligation to pitch in with some basic observations.

First, there is the observation that Job suggests in verse 15: "Did not he who made me in the womb make him? And did not one fashion us in the womb?" The other person whom Job has in mind is a servant, male or female. Job feels compelled to treat such a person with consideration because Job believes that in the end he and his servants are equal in their humanity. Both of them have come from God by the mystery of God's grant of fresh life. Both, therefore, must finally define themselves not as their own but as derived from an Other.

Certainly this observation remains as valid today as it was in Job's time. Certainly, people who wanted to find a basis for considering other human beings their radical equals would need only look to the common phenomenon of birth. What then makes a sentiment such as Job's so rare? Why is it that most of the systems underwritten in our society assume gross disparities in wealth and rights and, in fact, often increase them?

Job completely defines his situation in terms of his creaturehood. All that he is and has comes from God, so nothing very significant can be said about him without reference to God. In fact, one might answer Job's complaint that he is being treated unjustly by God on precisely these (his own) terms. Since God has given Job both life and goods, God can (for God's good reasons) take either life or goods away. Naked Job came into the world and naked he will leave. But even if Job cannot hear this personal thrust of his own appreciations of creaturehood, he certainly can hear overtones of the radical equality that obtains among all men and women. Most of our contemporaries either do not believe in a creator or have not taken to heart their professed acceptance of creation from nothingness. Consequently, they seldom reflect that at bottom they have no rights that God has not given them.

Now, suppose that God gives human beings rights to develop the earth, but not privatistically. Suppose that God places human beings in the world as a species that will flourish by cooperating, by considering the goods of the earth to exist for all of the earth's people. It would seem to follow that people believing in such a God and concerned to fall in with such a divine plan would think that all people ought to be provided necessities (food, shelter, clothing, medical care, education) before any people's hankering after luxuries got much attention. It would seem entailed that citizens of this persuasion would think of war as a gross violation of the radical equality and bedrock fellow-feeling encoded in all the members of the species and so would brand militarism pathological and preparations for war an industry that normally should be marginal.

Moreover, consider the place that money would tend to have were people to have taken their common creaturehood, their equal dependence on God for their birth, deeply to heart. Would money not appear as simply a convenience, a way of exchanging work and goods so that the whole family would receive proper care? And even if it became clear that people varied in their talents and their industriousness so that there was a valid basis for rewarding some people more than others, would it not seem highly disordered, completely forgetful of the Creator's fundamental provision of existence to all human beings, to develop an economy that paid more attention to the monetary profits of some people (say, the wealthy) than to the elementary material needs of other people?

We think we see this sort of disorder in the economies of other countries, for example, some countries of Latin America, where the top 10 percent of the population enjoys 60 or 70 percent of the gross national product (the profit if not the actual goods). But we have imbalances in our own domestic economy well worth considering, and they too will seem unbiblical to the extent that we follow Job in thinking that God has made all people equal by making them all wholly dependent creatures.

Any of us who even think along lines such as these soon find ourselves far from mainstream domestic economics and citizenship. Take the biblical indications of the radical equality of human beings to heart and you soon find that your country is light-years away from the Bible, Job, and Jesus. But just as ecological considerations suggest that we have our heads in the sand and are completely unrealistic about how God's creation runs, so considerations of the divine creativity suggest that we have made distinctions and prejudicial policies that simply do not square with how God made our species. By now such distinctions have gained institutional form and have come to shape education, taxation, and the military-industrial complex. It would be foolish to expect such arrangements to change in our lifetime. However, it would also be foolish to think that they have God's approval.

God has made us intelligent and responsible, so the systems we develop do have a general approbation in the divine blueprint. Yet God has also given us the capacity to see our utter dependence on our Creator for life, as verses such as verse 15 show, and from this capacity we could, if we wished, fashion a very different, a much more egalitarian, world order. To be sure, we should not call for revolutionary changes until we are sure that such changes will bring more good than harm. But theologians have the responsibility of bearing to their fellow citizens the fruits of their meditations on the nature of God. If theologians meditate on the nature of the biblical God seriously with an eye to economic and political entailments, they are bound to tell their fellow citizens that none of the present systems that ferry us toward war and perpetuate, indeed increase, our inflictions of injustice is justified in God's sight. The only economy God can approve is one structured by fair-sharing.

What is the relationship between sexual equality and peace in the home?

Why should one show the same compassion toward abused women and children and victims of AIDS?

What keeps us from making money just a means to serve all people a decent living?

27

Love

Song of Solomon 2:1–7

While most biblical scholars think that the Song of Solomon was originally secular love poetry, they debate its original date. A date after the Exile (after the mid-sixth century B.C.E.) is probable. A major reason that the rabbis finally included the Song in the Hebrew Bible was their sense that it fittingly allegorized the relationship between Israel and God. In other words, even if the Song originally described profane love, it might serve symbolists as a stimulating view of God's interaction with the chosen people. Christian mystics tended to take the Song as an allegory of the relations between the individual soul and God, seeing in its descriptions of withdrawal and return for delight a useful instruction in how God tends to lure the soul, purify it, and then unite it to divinity.

For our purposes the Song perhaps best serves as a reminder of how God views humanity—of what point of view probably frames the divine interests in peace and justice. It is presumptuous in the extreme to speak this way, of course, because no one is God's privy counselor, let in on the divine judgments and emotions. Still, by making certain writings Scripture the rabbis and church fathers cast the judgment that such writings were the best indication available of what God probably had in mind. Illumined by Jesus and the history of Israel, the Scriptures could be used in confidence that they would form readers in the dispositions necessary for salvation.

The Song of Songs tells us that romantic love not only is compatible with God but also is a prime revelation of the divine nature. The delight that our text describes is a valid analogy for the delight that the church should take in its God. The church is the bride of Christ, the body of Christ, the collectivity whom Christ regards as a lover. Unless there were strong emotional ties between the church and Christ, their unity of life and intention would not mean a great deal. Until the church loves Christ so much that it honors his concerns more than any temporal advantages of its own, it will not experience the full flourishing of the branches. So, for example, one might argue that until the church makes the longing of the Johannine Christ (John 17) for its unity more significant than the historical differences among its different families, it will not be the great sign lifted up for the nations. Were the church to long more for the pleasure of its Lord, long more to please its Lord, we would see less bickering and delay about ecumenical reunion.

The Song of Songs, therefore, has its rather sharp implications. Read as a symbolic expression of the emotional ardor that ought to obtain between people of biblical faith and their God, it condemns much of what we now produce as pale and lifeless. How many Christians in fact are sick with love of God, as verse 5 describes the beloved? How many churches must blush when they read verse 6, not because of the erotic overtones but because their own intimacy with God falls so far short of this ideal? Between Christ and his Body there ought to be intimacy on the model of sexual intercourse. Only that model can suggest the complete unity, compenetration, tenderness, surrender, and repair that worship and service ought regularly to produce.

If we read the apostle Paul with any seriousness, we realize that for him Christ was blazingly alive. The members of Christ had in Christ their most significant location or positioning. If they were shaped by being citizens of Corinth or Rome, they were more shaped by being members of Christ. If their temporal positioning in the mid-first century C.E. was significant, more significant was their living in the aeon when Christ had conquered death and poured forth the Spirit of divine life. Ephesians, most likely written by disciples of Paul, has the fullest development of the nuptial implications of Pauline ecclesiology, but all of the Pauline figures for the organic union between Christ and the church run to the same conclusion. Paul and other Christians no longer live a life of their own; they no longer have an independent existence worth bothering about because they have been taken up into the much more significant life of the Son.

The Book of Revelation also has a rich nuptial symbolism, and it too suggests that ardent love between Christ and the church should be natural. Where Paul concentrates on the present time (although he anticipates the consummation of history at the Parousia), John of Patmos concentrates on what goes on in heaven, where the deliverance of the saints from persecution already is being prepared. The Lamb who was slain is worthy to receive all honor and glory because he has accomplished the plan of the Ancient of Days and taken humanity to himself as a beautiful bride. The Spirit and the Bride say come, because they want this heavenly consummation to touch earth and time, bringing them the fulfillment for which they have been made and for which they long. So we see that the erotic poetry of Song of Solomon, with its implications that Israel is the lover of Yahweh, has equivalents, if not exact parallels, in the New Testament literature.

Verse 7 could even be read as a plea for patience between the lovers. Let the lover, God or people, rest until the time for renewed loving is right. Let history, the medium of the divine-human encounter, mature slowly and fully. In God's good time, the marriage will be fully revealed. Meanwhile, individuals and churches alike can console themselves that they live in the framework of a marriage that is still on its honeymoon.

Each time we gain a bit of peace, the love of God can come to us like an affirmation that renews our dedication. Each time we overturn some injustice, alleviate some suffering, lessen poverty or ignorance, we can take pleasure in the satisfaction that we have pleased the holy mystery to whom our faith binds us. Just as Exodus 3:13–17 suggests that we will learn about the God in whom we trust only by sojourning with God over time, so the risks we take for the sake of helping to advance God's kingdom can have a reward like that of a spouse who has labored hard for spouse or family.

Peacemaking and working for justice are not solitary ventures. We do them as members of Christ's Body, even when we stand at an outpost alone. Ideally, we have alongside us other members of Christ's Body, other branches of the vine. Ideally, we know a human, as well as a divine, collaboration and support. But the divine support, that is, the help of the Spirit, is the surer of the two collaborations, so we should make certain that it gets a large measure of our attention.

God is in love with humanity. Rosemary Haughton's fine book *The Passionate God* elaborates this theme in properly romantic terms. But Deuteronomic theology, which we have had more than a few occasions to criticize, already sensed this extraordinary fact. It was not because Israel was the greatest of the nations that God had showered the divine favor upon it. It was because of God's own inexplicable love. And as Judaism later interpreted the Song of Solomon, God showed yet another facet of the divine goodness in the romance with Israel. So at festivals the rabbis would take up the Torah that told the story of this romance and gave Israel guidance in its ways and would dance with it as a bride. So the wisdom that played before God at creation and constantly was God's delight had a feminine persona, and Christians applied many of the attributes of this wisdom to their Holy Spirit, whom they felt to be the force pouring forth the love of God into their hearts.

Virtually all of the kinds of love—parental love, the love of friends, of a teacher, of a king, of a healer—came to serve the theologians when they probed the relationship between humanity and God. But the bolder theologians, like the bolder mystics, gave a special place to the strongest of loves, the erotic romantic love that Proverbs 30:19 found too wonderful to comprehend. This is the love, after all, through which God brings forth new life. This is the love for which people leave father and mother. Fittingly, therefore, the song of this love is the Song of Songs.

Why did the rabbis and church fathers include the Song of Songs in the biblical canon?

What do the Song of Songs and Revelation suggest about puritanism and prudishness?

What is the significance of the equality of the partners to the erotic love of the Song?

28

Vanity

Ecclesiastes 1:1–9

The Book of Ecclesiastes testifies to the remarkable catholicity of the Hebrew Bible. The rabbis who sanctioned this collection of books as Scripture were not afraid of challenges to traditional faith. Job, as we have seen, questions deeply the divine justice. The writer of Ecclesiastes, or Qoheleth, as the Hebrew Bible calls him, represents faith at its most cynical, wondering whether any of our efforts in fact make a difference. Scholars note the strange vocabulary of Ecclesiastes, which contains numerous loan words from Persian, and tend to consider it quite a late work, probably composed after the Persian conquest of Babylon and the return of many Israelites to Judah.

My interest in this text is its expression of sentiments that many believers, if they are honest, have often felt. When we read the headlines year after year, we might wonder whether our leaders have learned anything from the past. The Soviets bumble into Afghanistan, although they have in the venture of the United States in Vietnam an object lesson in the futility of that sort of aggression. Our leaders in the U.S. escalate military involvement in Central America, although Vietnam, and many other situations in which we have supported corrupt regimes and alienated those most concerned to bring justice to the poor, shout that such escalation is folly. Farmers continue to vote for people whose policies are bankrupting them. The balance of payments worsens dramatically, and the budgets run at greater and greater deficits, but the voting populace is satisfied with a smile. Of what use are the efforts of church leaders and educators to raise up a critical electorate? Is the evidence not overwhelming that the majority have an active will not to know, an unquenchable appetite for soothing, manipulative pap?

Too often the situation is similar in the religious community. In many churches women still await full citizenship. In many headlines religious authorities show themselves more concerned about their own rights and privileges than the unification of Christ's church. Again and again narrow views of biblical inspiration condemn church groups to intellectual suicide, shouting that one cannot be critically intelligent and belong to their fold. Again and again, prudishness interferes with efforts to educate teenagers in a proper control of their sexuality or to educate adults in a proper control of alcohol and drugs. Many church leaders conspire with opportunistic politicians to moralize about such problems instead of mustering the resources and pragmatic will to cut the problems out at the root.

Rarely do the real figures about unemployment or the real figures about military expenditures or the real problem with projected defense shields get an honest airing. Rarely does nuclear winter's overshadowing of all of our futures penetrate the propaganda of Washington and become what it should be in any realistic capital—the first item on every agenda.

My colleague at the University of Tulsa, Grace Mojtabai, has produced a wonderful case study of one patch of religious vanity. Her book *Blessed Assurance: At Home with the Bomb in Amarillo, Texas* looks the craziness of fundamentalist reactions to nuclear armaments full in the face. Amarillo is home to Pantex, the final assembly point for all nuclear weapons made in the United States. It is also home to a large number of church people who think that nuclear holocaust might not be a bad thing, because it would bring God's just judgment upon the wicked world and take elect like themselves up into paradise. Grace, a sophisticated novelist of Jewish background, was so moved by the campaign of the Roman Catholic bishop in Amarillo, Leroy Matthiesen, to get workers to quit Pantex as immoral employment that she left New York and went to live in Amarillo to study the phenomenon on site. Bishop Matthiesen in fact persuaded only one worker to quit Pantex, and the community of Amarillo reacted to this threat to one of its main industries by cutting Catholic Charities from the rolls of its United Way.

Still, Grace deals with the many different viewpoints of Amarilloans gently and sympathetically. Finally, though, she cannot mask the horror she feels at the widespread accommodation to preparation for the Apocalypse. She senses that a very strange version of Christianity is often at work, one in which people have despaired about the ability of human beings to keep from destroying creation. She realizes that such people in effect discount the traditional Christian teaching about redemption. They do not really believe that Christ triumphed through the resurrection. They think that the essentials of salvation remain to be won. I shall return to Qoheleth and the despair induced by ignorance such as this, but first I need to say briefly a few things that Grace Mojtabai is too indirect or too polite to press forward.

First, the position of those eagerly awaiting nuclear Armageddon is heretical by any critical or traditional Christian accounting. It shows in particularly virulent form the ugliness and the mental imbalance that heresy has always imported. When people miss the mark of God's reality and fall into imbalance, they make one wonder whether God had fully calculated the costs of creation, incarnation, and redemption. What more could God have done than make human beings responsible for history, make the divine Word take flesh, and raise the Christ from the dead as Son of God and firstborn of a new creation? How could God have made it clearer that creation is dear to divinity and human beings draw from divinity the most self-sacrificing love? For putative believers to write off most of God's creation as fit for nuclear fire is a gross perversion.

Second, the fusion of such self-serving simplism with a ranting patriotism (which perhaps occurs in other places more dramatically than in Amarillo) compounds the heretical ugliness. We are the only people who have actually employed atomic weapons and thereby destroyed tens of thousands of lives. As a nation we had advanced technology sooner than other nations and so must be held accountable for the doomsday potential now ready and poised. Judgment, therefore, should begin with this household of God, ideally to the end that people would stream from their churches furious at the threats to God's creation and determined that the objectively massive sinfulness of preparing for nuclear war should come speedily to an end.

Qoheleth was discouraged because he saw injustice and immorality unaffected by his religion. He was discouraged because he knew that nothing in his own life would escape the grave. The stupidity of many of the people around him took away his will to work for change. The evil of other people made him wonder whether self-protection wasn't the only prudent course. In contrast, Jesus never let discouragement get such a hold on him. Although Jesus knew what was in human hearts, he continued to preach, to teach, to heal, and to put himself in peril. Ultimately, he suffered the abandonment of his closest followers and gave up his life for what seemed a lost cause. What sustained Jesus through such failure and pain? Why did he not come away thinking it all vanity?

The answer lies in Jesus' experience of his Father and the Spirit. Compare the God of Qoheleth with the God of Jesus and you have all the difference you need. Jesus felt that God was the most powerful force in existence. If you had forced Jesus to choose between the reality of God and the reality of the world, Jesus would have said it was the world that was the illusion. Certainly, Jesus must have suffered when he met rejection or when human beings revealed their depressing weakness. Certainly, Jesus did not die masochistically in an act that he enjoyed. And certainly the living Lord today must be horrified at the prospects of nuclear warfare. Yet for Jesus, even when we say "there is no way," the Spirit and the bride say "Come."

What does Qoheleth mean by "vanity"?

How does such vanity apply to the buildup of nuclear arms?

Why does a longing for nuclear rapture suggest heresy and mental imbalance?

29

Timing

Ecclesiastes 3:1–8

This famous text from the Preacher is beautiful in its own right, expressing as it does a profound faith in God's allowance and guidance of time. For people trying to advance the causes of peace and justice, it is also beautiful as an expression of what the New Testament might call sensitivity to the *kairos,* the pregnant, present hour. When we search the signs of the 1980s, what message from God seems the most pressing? When we consider the forces threatening human welfare and God's creation, what enemies emerge? Is this, as verse 8 might put it, a time for war or a time for peace? As the people of the third and fourth worlds might put it, is this a time for redoing the present distribution of the resources of the earth, or are present arrangements just and healthy?

I want to argue that this is a time for peace—indeed, that the call to peacemaking has seldom been more imperative. The reason, simply and obviously enough, is that we now have weapons that make any serious war horrifyingly destructive. The old justifications for war boiled down to a legitimate defense of a people's way of life and freedom against unwarranted aggressions. One could not legitimately initiate warfare, in view of its destructiveness, for the sake of more territory or even for the sake of righting old wrongs. One could, however, repulse unjust attacks and mount a countercampaign to disarm one's enemy as long as such efforts were likely to succeed and would not cause more harm than good. If the traditional theory of the just war is viewed as entailing such requirements, it emerges that a just war has always been hard to find.

Most of the wars that people have waged throughout history have not been justified, since they have been fought to expand territory and gain riches and power. Similarly, the religious wars have not been justified, since they pursued the compulsory acceptance of the aggressor's faith. In the rare situation of an evil as clear-cut as that of Hitler and Nazism, a first-rate theologian such as Dietrich Bonhoeffer could reason his way to the legitimacy of assassination. Even then the premise was that such an act could succeed and would hasten the end of hostilities. Defenses of any nation's military adventurism, therefore, face a great burden of proof. Be it the Soviet Union or the United States, actions that would initiate war have to be extremely well founded. By implication, actions that bring a nation closer to pushing the lethal buttons and pulling the lethal triggers similarly have to be extremely well founded.

All of this holds in the comparatively simple case of traditional, non-nuclear warfare. But, as many military analysts and ethicists alike now realize, the introduction of nuclear weapons with their unprecedented capacities for destruction changes the meaning of war so radically that past theory may well be irrelevant. Is there, nowadays, *any* good that would outweigh the evils of exploding large megaton bombs? Would even the defense of a nation's sovereignty positively outweigh the negative consequences of killing hundreds of millions of other human beings and wreaking on the earth's ecosystems incalculable and perhaps irreversible damage? Certainly, the burden of proof on those who would trigger nuclear weapons is a hundredfold heavier than that on those who would have initiated war even a hundred years ago. And it is arguable that the destructive potential in nuclear weapons now is such that the distinction between initiating war and retaliating (first and second strike) has narrowed considerably, perhaps to the point of irrelevance.

This being so, the implications for the nations' military postures and preparations for war also line up to be counted. If a nation may never morally explode large-scale nuclear weapons in view of the destruction of human life and the biosphere that such explosions portend, may a nation in good conscience threaten such an action? May we, that is, threaten and prepare to carry out actions that themselves are incompatible with the values imposed when we accept the gospel? On a small scale, we probably would agree that murder is wrong and that threatening murder—trying to coerce people by telling them that we are prepared to take away their life if they do not comply—also is wrong. What makes a large-scale use of such a tactic more acceptable? If using our nuclear weapons is probably wrong in all circumstances, how does preparing more and more nuclear weapons and rattling them as sabers pass muster in Christian conscience?

My opinion is that it does not pass muster, and so I judge the present time a time for peace. We have to reverse a demonic trend full of hatred for God, creation, and humanity if we are not to find in the future the era when God's gift of life is rejected as utterly as human beings can manage. We have to deal with enemies such as the Soviets in ways that keep them fully human in our imaginations. We must reject the stereotypes and myths that place our enemies outside God's pale.

True enough, past experiences caution against our trusting the Soviets, just as there are actions on our part that caution them to be wary of us. If they refuse their citizenry what we consider elementary freedoms and enslave many in political camps, we continue to be the only nation that has committed the enormity of atomic warfare. If they seem adventurous in the third world, concerned to foment instability and keep the fires of revolution burning, it is not hard to show that we are similarly adventurous, often abetting forces of repression and regimes that show only contempt for the poor.

Nothing in the profile of the two nations makes one the pure defender of all that is right. Simple honesty says that these two nations, like any other nation that one would want to bring forward, have sinned and fallen short of God's glory. I certainly prefer the general philosophy of the United States to that of the Soviet Union. My quarrels here are different from my quarrels there, for there I profoundly disagree on matters of principle while here I mainly lament the failure of politicians and people alike to deliver the justice and equal opportunity they like to laud. But in the perspective of true doomsday potential and under the tutelage offered by the non-ideological Spirit of God, I have to say that defense against Communism simply cannot be considered a sufficient rationale for our nuclear arsenal. Even without studying the depressing evidence that economic profit is a great engine driving our weapons industry (both our installations at home and our sales to nations abroad), I have to say that our national sovereignty, even our right to exist as this particular people and culture, does not come anywhere near the level of justification needed for threatening nuclear winter and the destruction of hundreds of millions of lives.

There is a time to speak in grim, even elegaic, tones about these matters, of course, and also a time to mock the fatheadedness that has gotten us into our present straits. There is a time to contemplate the most horrible of negative scenarios and also a time to affirm that even that would not exhaust the creativity of God. At all times, however, the cross of Christ is relevant, shifting the horizon of a Qoheleth. Where he could not see beyond the grave and so justified grabbing what decent pleasure one could, followers of Christ crucified and resurrected should be able to do better. Not being like pagans who have no hope, we ought to petition the Spirit for the wit to lead humanity back from the brink, back from dementia, away from the thoughtless worldly leadership that has proven so blind. The fact is that we will not have positive movement toward peace and the dismantling of our horrible weapons until we have a citizenry who trust more in God and less in bombs, who care more for the fruits of the Spirit and less about their wine cellars and stock portfolios. Our weapons are defending our greed. Now is the time to muster the faith to let both go.

Imagine the connection between a spirit graciously timing its approaches well and the feminine persona of biblical Wisdom in Proverbs 8 and 9.

How has the escalation of our destructive powers made warfare, and so aggression, untimely?

If this is not the time to let go of the weapons defending our greed, when is that time likely to come?

30

Wisdom

Wisdom of Solomon 10:9–21

Our final text comes from the Apocrypha. Most scholars think that the Wisdom of Solomon arose toward the end of the pre-Christian era, when wisdom literature abounded and Solomon was a useful authority to invoke. In our verses, the feminine persona of Wisdom is portrayed as the defender of such great biblical heroes as Jacob, Joseph, and Moses. To the author's mind, the fidelity they managed and the good results of their labors came from the guidance of God's counselor, from the guidance of the intelligence that gave God delight at the outset of creation when all order began. For our purposes, the Spirit of God who moderates wisdom in the Christian scheme of things comes into similar focus, inviting us to place our circumstances, our struggles to keep faith, and the outcome of our lives into her keeping.

In the previous meditation I focused rather starkly on nuclear warfare, trying to summarize the case against the buildup of our arsenals and for considering the present a time when peacemaking has become critically urgent. In this meditation let me focus on work for justice. Apart from preventing nuclear warfare, nothing seems more imperatively entailed by the gospel than changing the gross disparities in the nations' standards of living and offering the majority of the world's population a chance at a decent human existence—something they do not now have.

The figures on the various nations' consumption of the raw materials of the earth are fairly well known. For citizens of the United States, the most dramatic such figures are two, our percentage of the world's population (about 5 percent) and the percentage of the world's natural resources that we consume (about 35 percent). The latter figure varies from analyst to analyst, and it depends on how one understands both "natural resources" and "consumption." But none of the analyses that one can get from such international agencies as the United Nations or the World Council of Churches disputes that people in the United States live at a standard of consumption that cannot be extrapolated to the whole world. For us to consume at the level we now do, many other nations have to consume at least five times less per capita.

Even more crucially, for us to promote models of worldwide economic growth predicated on increasing consumption of natural resources to levels like our own runs contrary to ecological reality and sets poorer nations up for terrible disappointments. Temporary abundance of resources such as petroleum should not mislead us, nor should discoveries of new sources of nonrenewable resources. Wisdom lies on the path of redesigning the global economy so that we begin to live within the budget that nature itself affords us. Nature most definitely is not infinite in its resources of food and fuel. Nature has a carrying capacity that no technological ingenuity can leap over. Even without the political and military problems that weave their way through current discussions of the future of the biosphere, we have to take very seriously the rise of human population and the rise of more consumptive lifestyles. Together, they make scarcity, and so the likelihood of brutal conflict, more and more threatening.

I have previously furnished some of the bases for considering all of the earth's people radically equal in their humanity and so by nature entitled to an equal share of the goods of the earth. At the very least, this radical equality justifies the proposition one finds in Christian patristic literature: No one has the right to luxuries as long as anyone lacks necessities. One has only to compare the annual per capita income of the different nations today to realize that our present global economy grossly violates this proposition. The United States is not the wealthiest nation by this index, but we and many other Northern nations live at an indefensible level. People who would defend this level, often by arguing that we earned it fairly or that through our prosperity jobs and wealth are generated for other nations, cannot claim the backing of the Christian gospel.

The Jesus who appears in the New Testament is not likely to have much patience with abstract arguments when concrete people are suffering gross poverty, malnutrition, illiteracy, and the other evils that ruin life around much of the globe. Jesus said that we could know people and policies by their fruits. The only Christian defense for any economic policy is what happens to the wealth it generates. If that wealth actually gets to the full range of people involved, and makes them a community sharing burdens and rewards fairly, it bespeaks a good system. If that wealth does not circulate for the common good, supplying all with the bare essentials of a decent living and offering most a chance at some further prosperity, it bespeaks a system in need of overhaul. Certainly, Jesus counts good intentions and has patience for human foibles, but the Gospels give us no reason for thinking that Jesus does not fully stand behind his pragmatic criterion of actual fruits. So hungry children are going to count more than well-intentioned but addled bankers or bureaucrats. Sick people and people cut off from schooling are going to count more than people needing time in the Bahamas. The gross features of any economic analysis based on the New Testament are not hard to sketch. By such a sketch, the Northern nations should read Matthew 25 with fear and trembling.

So should we read Wisdom of Solomon 10. The heroes hymned in our text took direction from faith and their convenantal God. They had no insiders' newsletters, no Congressional Record, no intelligence reports circulated on a need-to-know basis only. True, communications were simpler in the days of the patriarchs, and one does not want to emerge a know-nothing, unappreciative of the theological value of increased knowledge of either God's universe or human events. But our current global injustices are not going to be solved by more factual information. They do not reside on the level of minor adjustments, tinkering with this foreign policy or toying with that rule of international banking. We suffer the discrepancies we do, and most of the consequent threats to our security, because people are not trying to work things out through a basic, simple wisdom that might be called godly.

Our major problem is not that nature will not produce enough to sustain five billion of us in good health, not that the nations cannot find the resources to educate their children, care for their elderly, find pen and paper for their mathematicians and flutes for their musicians. Our major problem is that we use our resources foolishly, wastefully, and greedily. The resources that the nations spend, virtually waste, on weapons and armies alone would remove most of the world's basic problems of hunger, illiteracy, and disease. The resources that a country such as our own spends on weapons and trivial recreation would clear our ghettoes and endow our institutions for basic research at five times their present rate. What drugs, alcohol, and teenage pregnancies cost us in any given year certainly could restore Appalachia and many a crushed inner city. The problem is not with our resources, not with our basic ability to draw from nature and human teamwork the essentials of a healthy life. The problem is the stupidity, the greed, and the lack of faith that keep us from doing what we might do rather easily.

This means that religion, for all its apparent puniness, is a vital player in any adequate scenarios for the year 2100. The religion I have in mind at this point is quite basic. Just as Jacob, Joseph, Moses, and Jesus thought God the only treasure worth worshiping, so must the nations come to think. Just as under God people felt constrained to fair-dealing, so must the nations come to feel. Wisdom is so living under God, in the presence of beautiful mystery, that destroying the earth or one's fellow human beings is unthinkable. Wisdom is realizing that peace and justice are the marrow of any culture, in comparison with which particular economic arrangements are quite secondary.

What is the tie between equalizing the nations' shares of the goods of the earth and preventing nuclear warfare?

How does the radical equality of all people in God's sight illumine the problems of redesigning the global economy so it will fit the limitations of nature's ecological systems?

How does God now ask you to express your religious convictions about peace and justice?

John Carmody is an author and theologian. He is currently a member of the religion faculty at the University of Tulsa.

Dr. Carmody's recent books include *The Quiet Imperative* and *Maturing a Christian Conscience* for The Upper Room, *Interpreting the Religious Experience* and *Exploring the New Testament* for Prentice-Hall, and *Bonded in Christ's Love* for Paulist Press.